Cusco, Peru

Cusco, Peru

James and Oliver Tickell
Photographs by Francesco Venturi

Tauris Parke Books, London

Cusco, quien te vio ayer
Y te ve ahora
Como no llora
?

Oh Cusco
he who saw you yesterday
And sees you now
How will he not weep?

(Maestro Gil Gonzalez Dávila, 31 March 1650)

This book is dedicated to the peoples of the Andes

The authors and photographer would like to thank the following for their help in the production of this book: Francesca Bristol, Roger de Bellegarde, Foptur, Antonio Aguilar Argandona, and La Manita Travel.

Published by Tauris Parke Books
110 Gloucester Avenue, London NW1 8JA
In association with KEA Publishing Services Ltd., London

Text © 1989 James and Oliver Tickell
Photographs © 1989 Francesco Venturi

Travel to Landmarks

Series Editor: Judy Spours
Designers: Sharon Ellis and Paul West
Original plans and maps by the Institute of Inka Research, Cusco; further drawing by John Hewitt
All photographs by Francesco Venturi except:
James Tickell, pages 52 (top), 62 (bottom left)

British Library Cataloguing in Publication Data
Tickell, James
    Cusco, Peru. — (Travel to Landmarks series).
    1. Peru. Cusco region — Visitors' guides
    I. Title 11. Series
    918.5'37

    ISBN 1-85043-172-8

Photosetting by Westerham Press
Colour separation by Fabbri, Milan, Italy
Printed by Fabbri, Milan, Italy

Contents

Map of the Cusco Region

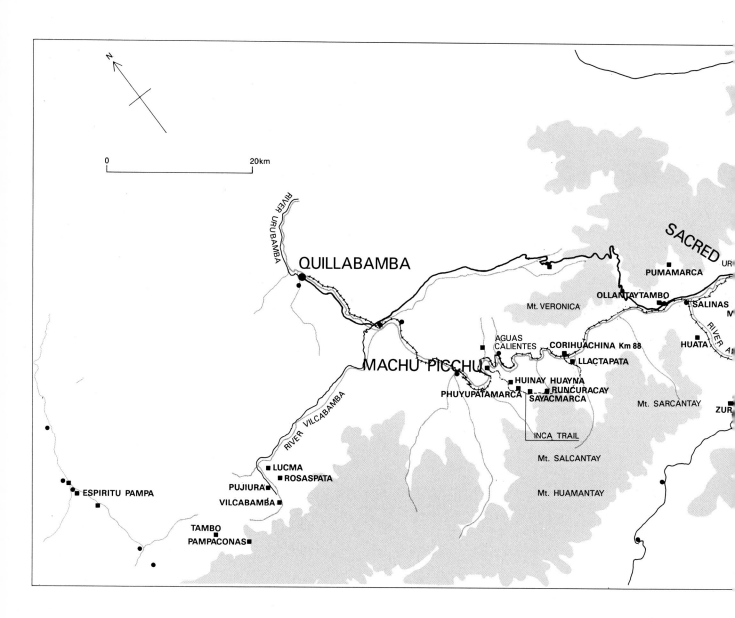

This map shows the places mentioned in the text, as well as a number of less accessible sites which are not covered. La Raya, the source of the Vilcanota river, is off the map to the right some twenty miles beyond Ragchi. The contour markings are approximate only, and much topographical detail has been omitted for the sake of simplicity.

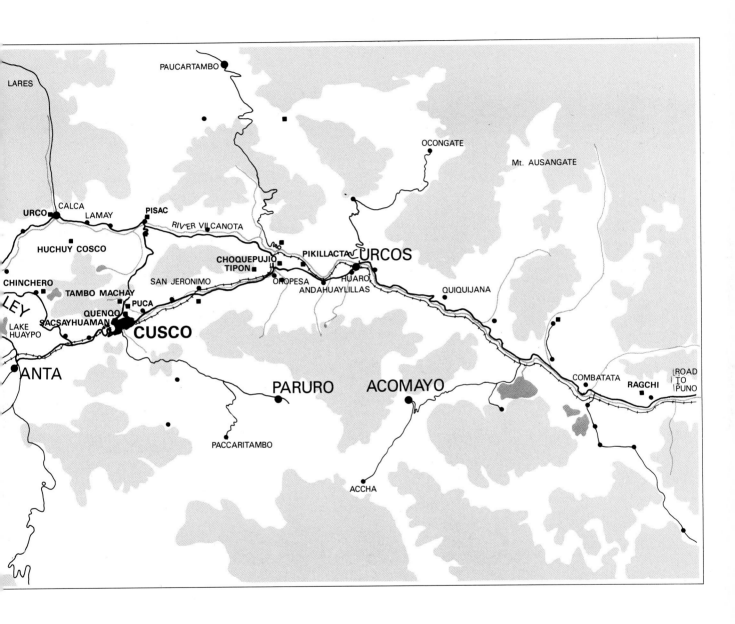

LARES

PAUCARTAMBO

OCONGATE

Mt. AUSANGATE

URCO CALCA LAMAY PISAC

RIVER VILCANOTA

HUCHUY COSCO

CHINCHERO

TAMBO MACHAY

PUCA

QUENQO

SACSAYHUAMAN

LAKE
HUAYPO

CHOQUEPUJIO
TIPON

PIKILLACTA URCOS

SAN JERONIMO

OROPESA HUARO

ANDAHUAYLILLAS

QUIQUIJANA

CUSCO

LEY

ANTA

PARURO ACOMAYO

COMBATATA RAGCHI

ROAD
TO
PUNO

PACCARITAMBO

ACCHA

Introduction

When the Inca Huayna Capac died in 1528, he was mourned by his tens of millions of subjects. His death was that of a god, the supreme ruler of an empire stretching three thousand miles up the western coast and mountains of the South American continent. The capital of Huayna Capac's empire and the centre of the Inca world was Cusco, a holy city of temples, gardens and palaces high in the Andes.

Far to the north, the Meso-American empires of the Aztecs and Mayas had already fallen to the Spanish conquistadors. Now they were planning new conquests, exploring the South American coast and gathering information about the power and wealth of the Incas. Huayna Capac knew little of this, having heard only rumours of the pale-skinned foreigners in their sailing ships. But his early death in an epidemic of an unknown disease, apparently smallpox, was a direct result of the Spanish presence on the continent, introducing new and devastating diseases. The worm had gone straight to the heart of the apple.

At the time of the Inca's funeral rites in Cusco, the very idea of the further devastation that was to follow was unimaginable. The empire of Tahuantinsuyo – 'the four quarters of the world' – had developed in isolation from other civilizations, and it knew of no power that could challenge the Inca. Yet within ten years of Huayna Capac's death his capital lay in ruins, his warriors had been butchered in their thousands, and Tahuantinsuyo was no more. The successor to the Inca's throne was Emperor Charles V of Spain, who was more interested in establishing European hegemony than in his new possessions on the American continents. Their main purpose for him was the provision of gold and silver bullion to finance European wars.

This book is about Tahuantinsuyo's capital city and the surrounding heartlands of the empire. It is also about the Spanish invaders who violently overthrew the ordered and stable world of Tahuantinsuyo, imposing their own religion and customs on the land, destroying most of what had gone before, but creating in the process the city that is Cusco today. The Spanish Conquest is the pivotal event of the book, referred to throughout, although no detailed account of its events is given. It would be pointless to try to summarize what others, notably John Hemming in his *Conquest of the Incas*, have done so well; the book list on page 127 gives details of this and of other useful books and guides. On page 126, a time chart gives a summary of Peru's

The Calle Loreto in Cusco, seen from the Plaza de Armas; it gives a good impression of what Cusco must have been like in Inca times. On the right are the remaining walls of Huayna Capac's palace, now the Jesuit church of La Compañía. The left wall belonged to the Acclahuasi, the House of the Sun Virgins, which became, appropriately enough, the convent of Santa Catalina.

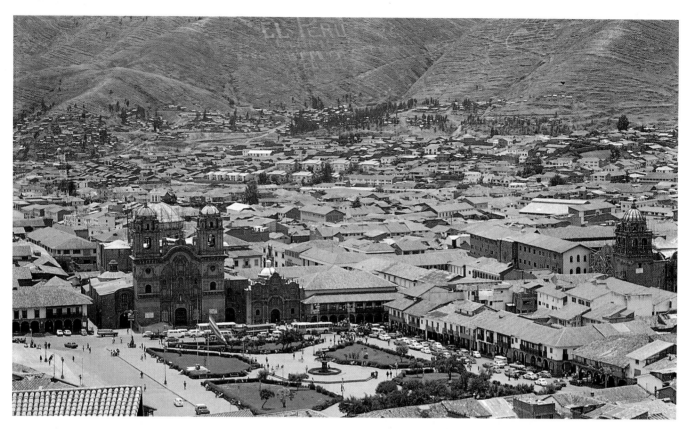

Opposite above, the Plaza de Armas in Cusco, the centre of the city since its foundation. The facing church is La Compañía, one of Cusco's most ornate Baroque churches.

Opposite below, one of the few intact systems of Inca agricultural terracing remaining, below the ruins of Pisac in the Sacred Valley.

Above, the Sacred Valley, seen from near the town of Maras. Before the Spanish Conquest, the now bare hillsides were covered in agricultural terracing and forest.

history from prehistoric times to the present day. The book aims to give an overview of Cusco's past and an introduction to the two very different societies which played on its stage, and, above all, to describe and evoke the places in and near Cusco, both as they were and as they are now.

Cusco today is capital to a Department of Peru of the same name, about the size of Scotland. This was the sacred centre of Tahuantinsuyo. The map on pages 6 and 7 shows the main part of the Department and the places mentioned in the text. The city lies at the centre in the fertile valley of the river Huatanay, surrounded on three sides by mountains. Chapter 1 is about the lost Inca city beneath the foundations of Cusco, and the ruins in its immediate surroundings.

South-east from Cusco, in the 'Quarter' of Collasuyu, rises a rugged, mountainous region, with the glaciers and peak of Ausangate reaching nearly 20,000 feet. Further south, across the 14,000 foot pass of La Raya, the mountains and valleys give way to the bleak high plain, the 'altiplano', which stretches across the border with the Department of Puno and beyond to lake Titicaca, mythical birthplace of the first Inca, Manco Capac, and into Bolivia. To the east and north, in the Quarter called Antisuyu, the mountains make their precipitous descent to the Amazon basin, largely unconquered at the time of the Spanish arrival.

At Rumicolca, not far south of Cusco, the river Huatanay joins the Vilcanota, the major river of the Department, which has its source near La Raya. It winds down from south to north, passing through the 'Sacred Valley', between the Inca sites of Pisac and Ollantaytambo. Chapter 2 follows the river from its source down to Ollantaytambo, taking in a number of the most accessible and important Inca and pre-Inca sites on the way. Past Ollantaytambo the river becomes a torrent that crashes down the forested ravines below the lost Inca city of Machu Picchu. Beyond, in the jungle plains, it joins the Amazon and flows eventually to the distant Atlantic Ocean.

Past Machu Picchu, several days' journey west over a mountain range, lie the ruins of Vilcabamba. Here Manco Inca and his heirs built a fortified city and resisted Spanish rule until long after the Conquest. Only in 1572 was their kingdom finally crushed. The story of these ruins and of their discovery is told in Chapter 3.

The first three chapters concentrate on the Incas; Chapter 4 turns to the Spanish

Above, restoration underway at Machu Picchu. Archaeologists here and at Ollantaytambo have created new ruins that the Incas would hardly have recognized.

Below, house at Ollantaytambo, of mud-brick and thatch on original Inca foundations. On the hillside above to the left is an Inca storehouse. There were once hundreds of these, dotted around the countryside, used to store supplies for time of famine or shortage.

and to the society they created after the extraordinary military achievement of the Conquest. It was the work of a handful of Spanish adventurers, just a few hundred strong, under the leadership of Captain Francisco Pizarro. The sheer courage and desperation of the invaders played a major part in their success. There were other factors on their side: alien diseases and the savage Inca civil war both weakened and demoralized the defenders; and the superior military technology of the Spanish was vital. But most important of all was the failure of Inca society to grasp the reality of the threat until it was too late.

Some of the Tahuantinsuyo's subjects welcomed their new rulers as liberators. They would soon discover that Spanish rule was harsher by far. It is important not to exaggerate the negative aspects of Spanish rule; nor to forget the honourable few who fought for the rights of the native population. Nevertheless, the Conquest was the beginning of a long nightmare of exploitation and oppression for the people of Tahuantinsuyo.

In Inca times Cusco was a centre of pilgrimage for Tahuantinsuyo. Just as a Muslim wishes to visit Mecca, so every subject of the Inca would wish to go to Cusco at least once in a lifetime. Now pilgrims still come to Cusco from the four quarters of the world, but in the name of tourism and not of religion. Most arrive by air, and their first sight of Cusco is a sea of red-tiled roofs, church domes and towers that give it the look of an Italian city. Hard to miss on second glance are the rows of mud-brick and corrugated-iron shacks spreading out from the centre, up the surrounding slopes, and covering the fields of the valley. Their inhabitants come from the hills, driven by hunger to abandon the land. Among the reasons for crop failure are flood, hail, frost, and drought, while accelerating soil erosion, over-grazing and the endless subdivision of land-holdings add to the problems. Without the food-stores or organizing genius of the Incas, and with their efficient agriculture destroyed by the Conquest, life for the Andean peasant today remains on the border-line between subsistence and starvation.

Cusco is a place where different cities are overlaid. Beneath it all lie the sleeping ghosts of Tahuantinsuyo. Inca Cusco, which the Incas visualized in the form of a puma, is less evident from the air, and no large parts of temples or palaces remain in the city itself. But walking around Cusco, traces of the Incas are everywhere.

The city of Machu Picchu, seen from the mountain of Huayna Picchu to the north of the site. Already abandoned by the time of the Conquest, Machu Picchu was never discovered by the Spanish and was lost for four centuries.

Many streets run the same course and bear the same names as they did five centuries ago. The foundations and supporting walls of many churches, mansions, even of ordinary houses and shops are of perfectly jointed Inca masonry. The stones of colonial buildings, quarried from Inca constructions, bear the marks of their original use.

Given the pervasive sense of their presence, it is strange how little we know about the Incas. They had no system of writing, and our knowledge of them therefore depends on post-Conquest chronicles (often biased against them) and on archaeological evidence. There are many theories, from the flying saucer and hang-glider variety to those based more firmly on the available evidence, but in every theory imagination has to play a substantial part. Maybe the best use for the imagination is to stand above Sacsayhuaman at dusk, looking out over Cusco, and try to retrace the body and tail of the puma that formed the capital of Tahuantinsuyo.

After the Conquest, Cusco lost its importance as the centre of a civilization, though it became a major centre of religious and decorative arts. Its 'long sleep' was broken only by earthquakes and the occasional indigenous uprising. The discovery of Machu Picchu in 1911 by the American archaeologist Hiram Bingham was the single event that propelled Cusco into its present position as an archaeological and touristic centre.

Quite understandably, many visitors arrive and leave without realizing that there is more to be seen in the city and department of Cusco than the standard three days of churches on the main square, Sacsayhuaman, the principal Inca sites in the Sacred Valley, and Machu Picchu. But even to do full justice to the museums, churches and Inca remains within easy walking distance of the city centre could take weeks rather than days. Further beyond, there is hardly a hillside or valley without some evidence of Inca or pre-Inca terracing, irrigation systems, or other constructions. Any village church may hold exquisite and unknown canvases or murals from the Cusco School of painting. Much of this is accessible to visitors who are ready to go a short distance off the beaten track.

In more remote areas, ruined cities larger than Machu Picchu have been detected from satellite pictures, but in the absence of resources for their exploration they are destined to remain hidden for many years. The whole countryside is criss-crossed

Mural painting in the church of Huaro, a small village to the south of Cusco. It was painted at the end of the eighteenth century by an indigenous painter, working under Spanish direction. Many of the murals have Death as their theme – here Death in the shape of a skeleton is cutting down the Tree of the Good Life, helped by a devil pulling the branches with a rope. Beneath the tree, Jesus is tolling a bell, calling on sinners to repent before it is too late.

by Inca stone highways; again, satellite pictures are just revealing the full extent of the network, which ran for many thousands of miles, linking all the major centres of the empire. But no one today can ever fully appreciate the greatness of Tahuantin-suyo, for, in the words of Sir Clements Markham, writing early this century:

It was destroyed by the Spanish conquest, and the world will never see its like again. A few of the destroyers, only a very few, could appreciate the fabric they had pulled down, its beauty and symmetry, and its perfect adaptation to its environment. But no one could rebuild it . . . and the unequalled fabric disappeared for ever.

Cusco City Centre

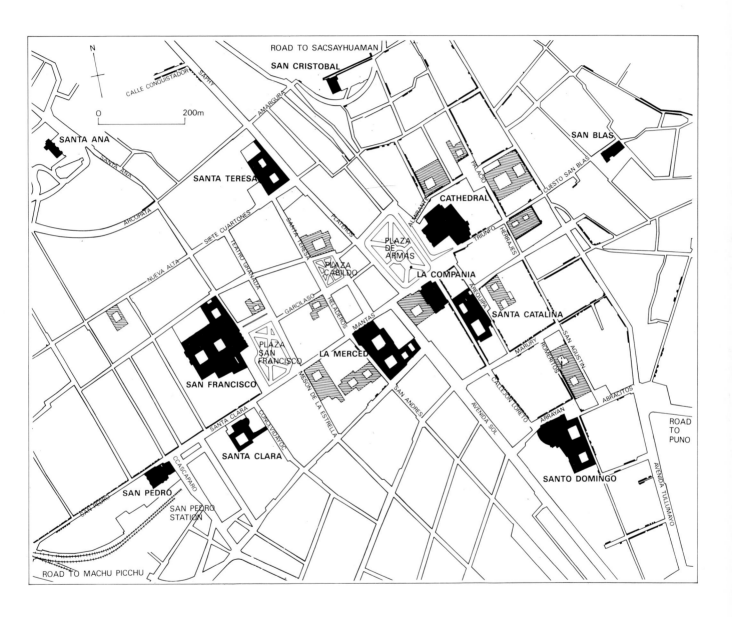

*The historical centre of Cusco, showing the main places of interest,
and street names. Where a city block has bold lines, this shows the
existence of Inca stonework.*

Tahuantinsuyo

1

When the Spanish arrived in Cusco, they saw the greatest city the continent of South America had ever known. It had perhaps as many as 125,000 citizens; this population level was not reached again until the 1970s. About 16,000 lived in the ceremonial and religious centre, around the square of Huacaypata (Holy Square or possibly Square of Warriors), now the Plaza de Armas. These were the royal families, the priests and temple attendants, and those who served them. Another 50,000 or so, the ordinary people of Cusco, lived in settlements just outside the centre. Further out across a stretch of fields 'satellite' villages were occupied by a more transient population coming from the four quarters of the empire. Above the city, on a hilltop to the north-west, was the great fortress-temple of Sacsayhuaman, almost a town in its own right, its three towers dominating the skyline.

The empire itself had existed for less than a century, but the Inca presence in Cusco dated back to about AD 1000, the approximate date of Cusco's foundation by the Inca Manco Capac. Our only knowledge of the first Inca comes from creation myths told to Spanish chroniclers after the Conquest. Several versions exist, with Manco Capac and his sister queen variously emerging from the waters of lake Titicaca, or from caves in a hillside at Paccaritambo, to the south-east of Cusco. There is agreement, though, on some key facts, which seem to indicate that Manco Capac assumed leadership of the Inca people, killing a number of his brothers and marrying his sister in the process. He then led the Incas north, taking several years to reach the valley of Cusco. There, Manco Capac thrust his golden staff into the ground: when it sank deep in the fertile soil he knew that this was to be the Incas' home. The palace that he built for himself was later to become Coricancha (Enclosure of Gold) and the chief Temple of the Sun. By popular legend he built another palace at Colcampata, below Sacsayhuaman.

Even less is known about Manco Capac's first four successors. Doubtless the religion and the administrative and agricultural systems that were later to serve the Incas so well were evolving during their reigns. Almost certainly there were wars with neighbouring tribes, and contacts with the more powerful rival kingdoms of the region. In any event, there were no great conquests, and the Incas remained a small if prosperous tribe, occupying a territory in the valley of Cusco no more than fifty miles across.

A close-up of one of the snakes on the wall of the Casa de las Sierpes. For the Incas the snake was a symbol of learning and intelligence, and the motif commemorates the site's original use as a school for the education of the sons of Inca nobles.

An interesting feature of Inca creation myths is that they seem to indicate absolutely no knowledge of preceding people and cultures. This is in part due to a deliberate re-working of history, designed to legitimize Inca rule and to reinforce the links between state and religion. But the Incas were probably also largely ignorant of the earlier great empires of the region, the older one based at Tiwanaku (also Tiahuanaco) near lake Titicaca, and the second at Wari, near modern Ayacucho. Both in turn had held sway over Cusco. Our knowledge of these and other early civilizations is based entirely on archaeological evidence, but what we see is impressive – there are fine, sophisticated weavings from Paracas, advanced ceramics from Moche, the enormous carved monoliths of Tiwanaku, and much more. The Incas have to be seen in the context of the rich and ancient cultural traditions of the region. As the story of their subsequent expansion shows, the particular genius of the Incas was not so much creative as in adaptation, administration and military conquest.

The reign of the sixth Inca, Inca Roca, saw the creation of a highly disciplined militaristic state. He also created the enduring division of the noble and royal Inca ayllus (clans) into 'upper', Hunan, and 'lower', Hurin; each had their own part of the city. Inca Roca is generally credited with the foundation of Cusco as a true city, draining the marshy areas, channelling the rivers Huatanay and Rodadero, and using their waters for irrigation in the valley.

Although the Inca kingdom expanded under Inca Roca, the eighth Inca, Viracocha, was the first to undertake the assimilation of conquered tribes. He placed administrators among them, backed up by Inca garrisons, and forced the use of the Quechua language, still in use over most of the former empire. The pace of conquest remained slow until he took advantage of local wars to take over a large area around lake Titicaca. Just after this, a major threat to the Incas emerged in the shape of the Chanca, a rival tribe whose territory lay to the west of Cusco. When they felt that Viracocha was growing weak with age, they marched on Cusco with such a powerful army that most of the Inca nobility barricaded themselves into a fortress near Pisac.

However, two of Viracocha's sons and a small band of determined followers decided upon a last ditch defence of Cusco. Under the inspired leadership of the youngest son, Cusi Yupanqui, they beat off the superior forces of the Chanca, who retreated to a nearby valley to prepare for a counter-attack. A further sortie led by

Above, detail of the Inca wall at Colcampata, near the church of San Cristóbal. Supposedly built by Manco Capac, the inferior quality of the stonework is a sure sign that it dates from a later period.

Below, details of Inca polygonal masonry in the wall of the palace of Inca Roca, subsequently the Archbishop's Palace and now the Museum of Religious Art, about two blocks north-east of the Plaza de Armas. The stone on the left is the famous twelve-sided Great Rock, Hatunrumiyoc in Quechua, which gives the street its name. The one on the right, although less widely featured, has fourteen sides; technically, both are superb achievements, fitting perfectly into the wall and leaving no gap. Outside Cusco there are various examples of polygonal blocks with thirty or more angles, but for their precision these two are the most impressive examples of polygonal masonry to be found.

Above left, the circular wall of Coricancha, the Golden Enclosure, which housed the principal Temple of the Sun. The construction dates to the time of Pachacutec and is probably the finest surviving example of the regular coursed style of rectangular masonry. The circular plan is in itself a rarity. Above is the church of Santo Domingo, the geometrically patterned woodwork of the balcony showing signs of Moorish influence.

Above right, some of the 'Inca' stonework in Cusco actually dates from after the Conquest. It is not always easy to tell it from the real thing, but good clues are the later use of mortar and of vertical as opposed to slightly sloping construction. The wall on the right of the picture, of the Casa de las Sierpes in the Plaza Nazarenas, is certainly post-Conquest. Authorities disagree about the wall on the left, but there are almost no other examples of this kind of relief carving on Inca walls.

Below left, this doorway, at Calle Choquechaca no.339, is certainly of Inca construction. It is now part of a colonial mansion, but the double jamb indicates that it was once the entrance to a very sacred place; in this case, the original purpose is unknown.

Below, right, corner detail on Calle Loreto of the walls of Acclahausi, the House of the Sun Virgins, which housed beautiful young women selected from all over the empire to become priestesses or royal consorts. In the 1950 earthquake much stonework was dislodged from the colonial building on the site, revealing unknown Inca walls, and it is certain that much more remains hidden.

Cusi Yupanqui, in which he killed the enemy chief in hand-to-hand combat, finally destroyed the Chanca armies. The assimilation of the Chanca territory into the growing Inca domain soon followed. Cusi Yupanqui then took power, against his father's wishes but with wide support, assuming the name Pachacutec. The year was 1438.

Under Pachacutec, the empire's expansion was explosive. While the Inca dominion already extended hundreds of miles to the south-east, independent neighbours, many of them old rivals, remained within a day's march of Cusco. These were Pachacutec's first targets. Next he conquered the mountainous regions around Cusco, before adding the lands near lake Titicaca. Wherever possible, tribes and nations were persuaded to accede to the empire without a fight – and many did. As the process of conquest and assimilation spread, so the name Tahuantinsuyo (Land of the Four Quarters) came to be applied by Pachacutec to his fast-growing empire.

In the same way as the Spanish Conquest was later to be assisted by the impressive infrastructure of Tahuantinsuyo, so the Inca expansion was made possible by the assimilation of existing kingdoms, complete with their administrations, agricultures and religions, with minimum disruption. Of the known Inca world only Antisuyo, the Amazon, remained largely unconquered; even so, its fringes produced many valuable commodities for the empire, including coca leaves and other medicinal plants, timber, exotic fruits and gold.

The scale of military operations was growing so huge that the Inca army's numbers were swelled by conscripts from defeated areas. This gave rise to concern about the loyalty of the troops, and rebellion by some newly conquered population was always another possibility. To guard against these risks, Pachacutec introduced the practice of 'mitima': settlements of loyal subjects would be placed in newly subjugated territories, while the original inhabitants were moved to areas where they could be more easily controlled. On the whole, this system was effective, but maybe a more important reason for the stability of the empire was that its rule was just and the tributes far from harsh. Indeed, membership of what one scholar calls the 'Pan-Andean co-Prosperity Sphere' of Tahuantinsuyo brought many benefits, including security against hunger or foreign attack, and the largest price to be paid was the loss of liberty.

Pachacutec chose his youngest son, Tupac Yupanqui, as his successor. But well before his accession, Tupac Yupanqui was maintaining the pace of expansion, carrying the boundaries of the 'Quarter' of Chinchasuyu beyond Quito, now capital of Ecuador, then working his way back down the coast. On his enthronement, a series of campaigns conquered the southerly coastal nations, some of the troublesome jungle tribes of Antisuyo and the highland region of modern Bolivia and northern Chile. Tupac Yupanqui thus became the ruler of an empire that stretched nearly the whole length of the Andes from central Chile to northern Ecuador, occupying an area of some 350,000 square miles.

Imperial Cusco

While Tupac Yupanqui was expanding the empire to the north, his father Pachacutec turned his attention to administration, the performance of religious ceremonies, and the erection of the golden-clad temples and palaces of Cusco. His wish was to build an imperial capital worthy of Tahuantinsuyo. The resulting transformation of Cusco from the centre of a tribal kingdom into a great city is often referred to as the 'second foundation of Cusco'. As well as Cusco itself, Pachacutec was responsible for the reconstruction of Sacsayhuaman, another vast project. Most of Cusco's older buildings were destroyed or rebuilt, and the villages within a six mile radius cleared, with their inhabitants sent to more remote regions. Pachacutec replanned the city, using as his inspiration the shape of a great puma, as shown on page 104. A 50,000 strong workforce, mostly drawn from conquered peoples, carried out the rebuilding over a period of twenty years.

Cusco was conceived by the Incas as the centre of the world – the word Cusco means 'navel' in Quechua. The four quarters of Tahuantinsuyu met in Huacaypata, the huge main square, from where roads radiated to the farthest points of empire. Huacaypata, together with the slightly smaller adjacent square of Cusipata (Square of Joy), across the river Huatanay, provided a place for enormous gatherings. With the stone walls of Inca palaces on three sides, Huacaypata was used for formal occasions, while Cusipata was for celebrations. Spanish chronicler Miguel de Estete's account of the coronation of the puppet Manco Inca in 1533 gives an idea of the nature of the festivities enjoyed there:

Plan of Cusco in Inca times, with the shape of the great puma high-lighted, and showing the division between Hunan and Hurin Cusco.

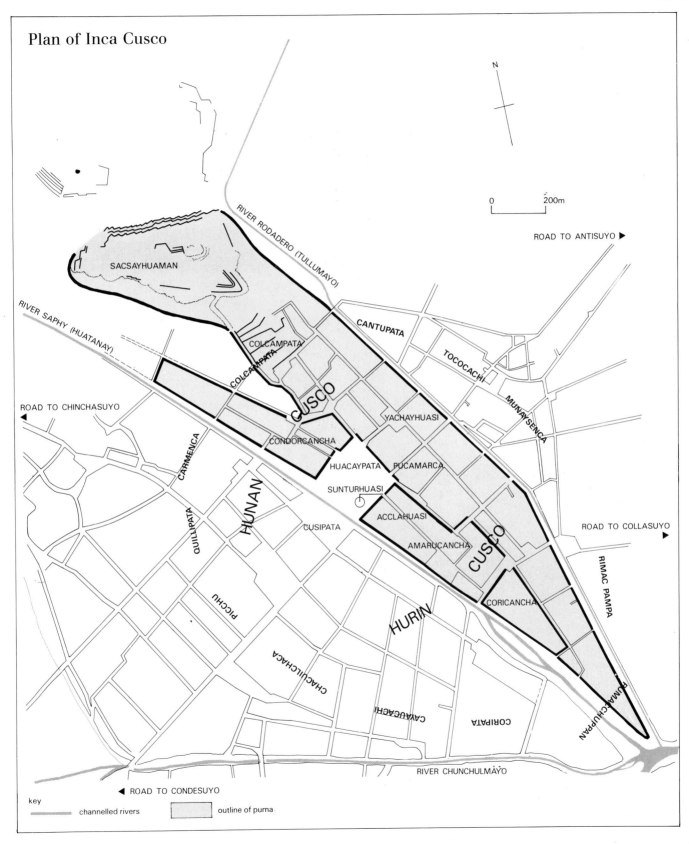

Plan of Inca Cusco

key
— channelled rivers   outline of puma

The foundations of the central tower, 'Muyuc Marca', at
Sacsayhuaman; the other two towers had rectangular plans. The
diameter of the outside ring is 75 feet; the inner ring is now known as
the eye of the puma. Muyuc Marca had four storeys with windows
looking out over Cusco, and was apparently used when the Inca
stayed at Sacsayhuaman.

There were so many people, and both men and women were such heavy drinkers, and they poured so much into their skins – for their entire activity was drinking, not eating – that two wide drains . . . which emptied into the river beneath the flagstones ran with urine throughout the day from those who urinated into them, as abundantly as a flowing spring.

Most of Huacaypata survives to this day as the Plaza de Armas, but Cusipata was soon built upon by the Spanish, with just the small Plaza Regocijo and the tiny Plaza Mantas remaining as open space. Nothing remains of the Inca armoury of Sunturhuasi, a cylindrical tower four floors high in the southern part of Huacaypata, the tallest building in old Cusco.

The planning of the city was carried out using clay models, made to scale. Most of the buildings in the centre were of single-storey construction, with foundations and lower walls of rough stone, main walls of classic Inca cut and fitted masonry, and upper walls of adobe, sun-baked bricks of earth and straw. Roofs were made of wood and thatch, as the use of tiles was unknown. Outside the reserved central area, settlements were less carefully laid out, and the buildings were of adobe or rough stone set in clay, once again with thatched roofs. In these areas only the temples and shrines had cut and fitted stonework, perfectly joined without mortar in the typical Inca style. Classic Inca stonework could be of one of two main types, rectangular and polygonal. There is some evidence that earlier buildings were generally of polygonal masonry, while later the preference was for the regular, coursed rectangular style, but there is no firm rule as the two styles were used concurrently.

Pachacutec left many great buildings in Cusco. His own palace, Condorcancha, later to become Francisco Pizarro's Cusco residence, occupied an entire block on the north-west side of Huacaypata. All that remains of it are a few walls, now part of hotels and restaurants. Manco Capac's palace at Colcampata was probably rebuilt by Pachacutec, who called it Llactapata (Village on the Hill). In addition, he may have built Yachayhausi, the school in which the sons of Incas and noblemen were educated. This site is now occupied by the Nazarene Convent and the Church and Seminary of Saint Anthony, on the small Plaza Nazarenas to the north-east of the Plaza de Armas. Fine Inca walls and ceremonial portals remain visible.

Pachacutec enlarged Coricancha; the rectangular masonry that survives as the foundations of the church and convent of Santo Domingo dates to this time. Corican-cha also served as Cusco's principal observatory: solstices and equinoxes were known by solar alignments with towers built on the surrounding mountains. One of Corieancha's greatest wonders was its garden, which contained llamas, human figures, flowers and plants exquisitely made from gold and silver, while the temple itself was covered with sheets of gold. Needless to say, none of these wonders survived the Conquest. The sheets of gold went to ransom the Inca Atahualpa from Pizarro, while conquistador Diego de Trujillo took the balance. In his own account, the high priest greeted his entry with the words: 'How dare you enter here! Anyone who enters here must fast for a year beforehand, and enter barefoot bearing a load!'. He paid no attention, and soon the gold and silver figures were on their way over the Andes for smelting down to ingots. Only the enormous golden image of the sun, the Punchao, is believed to have escaped, so well hidden that it has not been found to this day.

Pachacutec's successor, his son Tupac Yupanqui, carried on the rebuilding of Cusco and Sacsayhuaman. His main new project was the palace of Pucamarca on the east corner of Huacaypata; many of the walls are still standing, and some can be seen inside Cusco's present tourist office. He is also thought to have built Acclahausi, the House of the Sun Virgins. The high outer walls of Acclahausi are still standing, in Calle Loreto and Calle Arequipa, just south-east of the Plaza de Armas. In the 1950 earthquake much colonial stonework was dislodged to reveal unknown Inca walls, and it is certain that much more remains hidden.

After the death of Tupac Yupanqui, his successor Huayna Capac does not seem to have carried out any major building works in Cusco, apart from the usual practice of building his own palace, Amarucancha, where the University of Cusco now stands.

Sacsayhuaman and beyond

Pachacutec's greatest project was the reconstruction of Sacsayhuaman (Satisfied Falcon or possibly Royal Falcon). The ruins are the only major site near Cusco, and were linked to Huacaypata by a short Inca road, the last part of which still survives from just beyond the church of San Cristobal near Colcampata. Sacsayhuaman

The great zig-zag walls of Sacsayhuaman, seen from the esplanade.
To quote Pedro Sancho, a companion of Francisco Pizarro: 'These
walls . . . are built of stones so large that nobody who saw them
would think they had been laid there by human hands — they are like
great mountain crags.'

Above, monumental doorway at Sacsayhuaman. The lintel is not the original – the stone is of a different type, and does not fit cleanly. It was placed there recently by enthusiastic would-be restorers.

Below, an area of volcanic outcrops to the north of Sacsayhuaman, used as a quarry for the construction of buildings in other parts of the site.

stands on a hill some 500 feet above the city to the north-west. A slope beneath a single wall falls steeply down to Cusco, and at the top stood the towers that so impressed the Spanish. On the other side of the towers are the three famous parallel zig-zag walls, made of huge boulders and running for nearly a third of a mile from east to west. Beneath their terraces is a wide esplanade, to its north a small hill known as Suchuma (or Rodadero), covered by the foundations of buildings. Beyond Suchuma, excavations are still underway in several zones, and the findings indicate that even before the Incas the site had long been used.

The foundations of the three towers were only uncovered in 1934. The towers had their own stores and water supplies, and were linked by a series of tunnels. All around them were temples, observatories and other buildings. On some of the walls were gold tablets, removed by the conquistadors, who demolished the towers and used the stone in the construction of colonial Cusco.

Almost all the buildings of Sacsayhuaman suffered the same fate at some stage – as late as the 1930s the site was still being used as a quarry. But the huge stones that make up the inner zig-zag walls were unmovable and remain to this day. The largest of the stones is 28 feet high and estimated to weigh over 360 metric tons. We can only guess at how they were transported, positioned and tailored to a precise fit. But even using the technologies of the time – ropes, sleds, rollers, levers, and the methodical chipping away of one stone by another harder one – unlimited, well-organized manpower could achieve amazing feats.

This observation has not prevented the development of other, more exotic theories. Some guides at Sacsayhuaman will happily explain that the Inca priests had perfected the art of levitating stones, and that a liquid made from jungle herbs was used to soften the stone to the consistency of putty. There is also a theory that the Incas were preceded by an earlier 'megalithic' civilization, responsible for positioning the giant stones at Sacsayhuaman, Tiwanaku and elsewhere. This is supported by an Inca myth that speaks of a time when the earth was illuminated by the moon and inhabited by strange men who could move stones by force of will. But current archaeological thinking places the 'megalithic' constructions within the later Inca period.

Pachacutec created Sacsayhuaman in its later form, defining the final outline that

Two pictures of the large carved rock at Sacsayhuaman known as the 'Throne of the Inca', although for no very good reason. Its true purpose is not known, although we can be certain that it had some important ceremonial use.

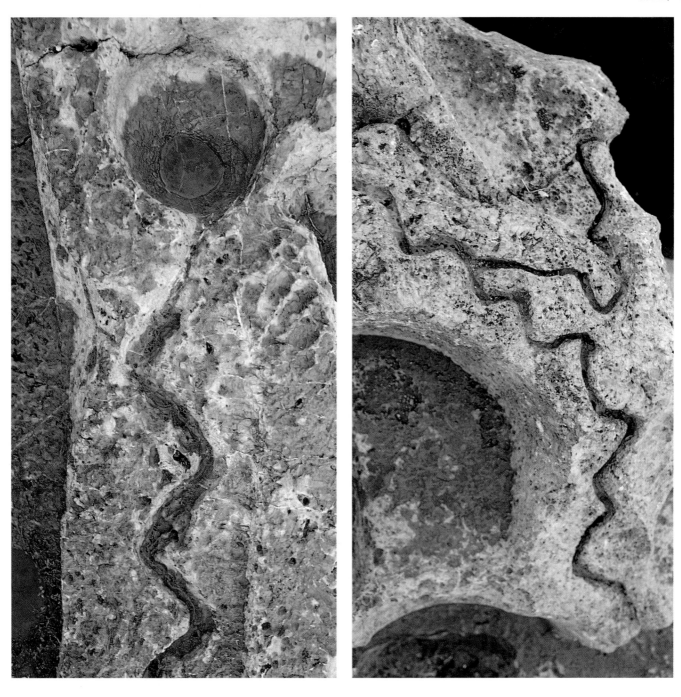

Zig-zag channels carved into the rock of the huaca at Quenqo. These may have been used to carry the blood of sacrificed llamas and other animals – unlike the Aztecs of Mexico, the Incas are not thought to have practised human sacrifice. The channels are near the double Intihuatana.

we see today, built over older structures. His son Tupac Yupanqui also enlarged the structure, concentrating on the buildings within the walls. The original structure was certainly defensive – in the early days, hostile tribes were never far away. But by the time of Pachacutec there was little threat from foreign powers in the valley of Cusco. He was probably developing Sacsayhuaman for use as a religious centre, expanding the temples and building up the famous zig-zag outer walls as a monument to the God of Lightning.

But whatever the true purpose of Sacsayhuaman, the Spanish were in no doubt that it was a dreadful fortress. Indeed, the first time we know it was used as a fortress was against the Spanish, in the Manco Inca's Great Rebellion of 1536. This nearly achieved its objective of driving the Spanish out of Cusco, though in spite of the superior numbers and courage of the Inca troops, the rebellion collapsed. When Sacsayhuaman was finally occupied by the Spanish, its 1,500 defenders were put to the sword, and became prey for huge flocks of condors.

To the north and east of Suchuma are a number of natural rock formations, including a labyrinth under a vast carved stone, its passages thought to have been carved out by the action of underground streams. Nearby are a series of extraordinary rock-slides, probably caused by the movement of glaciers in prehistoric times. Further away is the recently restored 'amphitheatre', the true purpose of which is unknown.

The asphalt road that passes Sacsayhuaman on the way to Pisac passes near three lesser but interesting sites, Quenqo, Puca Pucara and Tambo Machay. Further off the beaten track, linked by Inca pathways, are any number of unrestored sites, including irrigation works and more of the carved outcrops ('huacas' – the word also means 'sacred place') that were often at the centre of Inca shrines.

Quenqo, about a mile from Sacsayhuaman, is an especially large huaca. Originally, it was surrounded by temple enclosures, ritual baths and so on, but all that remains is what the Spanish could not easily destroy, including the base of a double sundial carved into the rock. In Quechua this is called an Intihuatana, a word coined by archaeologists meaning 'hitching post of the sun'. These are found in most Inca sites, and probably supported sophisticated instruments, none of which has survived. Further down from the main rock formation is an amphitheatre, dominated by a monolith nearly twenty feet high, a huaca in its own right. Formerly it was covered with sacred carvings, but these were disfigured by Spanish 'extirpators of idolatry'.

To the east up an Inca road is the huaca at Susurpuquio. This huge, rocky outcrop has a deep split which has been enlarged into a tunnel. On top are many ledges and carvings of animals, including a pair of condors and llamas. It was by the stream at its foot that the young Pachacutec, before going to battle against the Chanca, had his legendary vision in which the future glories of the empire were revealed to him by the Sun God.

About four miles along the road from Quenqo are the ruins of Puca Pucara. The original name is not known, but Puca Pucara means 'Red Fort'; in fact, the site is not now thought to have been a fort in more recent Inca times, nor is it clear why it should be called red. The buildings are grouped around a number of enclosures surrounding a hilltop. The stonework is unremarkable and its most likely use was as a staging post for travellers. Nearby, across the road, is the site of Tambo Machay, at the head of a small valley. The site consists of three terraces of fine classic Inca stonework, connected with stairs. A stone channel runs across the second terrace, carrying water from an unknown spring within the hillside. At the foot of the terracing, a double stream falls out over the bathing place. Opposite the terracing are the remains of a small circular tower, probably used for signalling to Puca Pucara.

After the death of Tupac Yupanqui, his son Huayna Capac became Inca. The date was probably 1493, just one year after Christopher Columbus first arrived in the Americas. The reign of Huayna Capac was long and successful, though without the military glories of his two predecessors. There was by now little scope for expansion, and the communications system, despite the system of roads that connected every corner of the empire, had become rather stretched. Nevertheless, he conquered warlike tribes as far north as the present Ecuador-Colombia border, creating the greatest ever extent of Tahuantinsuyo. He preferred the wetter climate of the northern highlands, and spent the last years of his life based in Quito with his illegitimate but favourite son, Atahualpa, while his royal sons stayed in Cusco.

Huayna Capac had intended to divide the empire, giving Atahualpa the northern

Above, the beautiful water temple of Tambo Machay, thought to have been used for ritual bathing by the Inca.

Below, the underground chamber at Quenqo known as the Chamber of Sacrifices; the blood ran down to here from the channels above. The rock table may have been used for embalming the corpses of the nobility; beneath it is a deep gully into which, by popular legend, condemned criminals were thrown to the mercy of venemous snakes.

kingdom of Quito, while his eldest son Ninan Cuyuche was to rule the remainder of the empire from Cusco. But in 1525 Tahuantinsuyo was struck by a terrible epidemic of an alien disease, probably smallpox. This carried away the Inca, together with much of his court, Ninan Cuyoche and an unknown though enormous number of his subjects.

Soon after Huayna Capac's death, another royal son, Huascar, was enthroned as Inca in Cusco. But suspicion reigned between Huascar and his ambitious half brother, Atahualpa. Ambassadors were executed, and it was not long before the two were at war. The brothers met in a series of battles in all of which Atahualpa was victorious. Finally, Huascar's army was ambushed in a ravine, and the Inca taken captive. Atahualpa's triumphant army advanced on Cusco, which declared allegiance to the new Inca following an assurance that no reprisals would be taken. But Atahualpa had different ideas. From his encampment at Cajamarca he ordered the execution of Huascar's entire family and supporters – over eighty of his children alone were killed, their corpses strung up on poles along the highway from Cusco. Huascar was compelled to watch the dreadful slaughter, which had a shattering effect on the morale of the nobility and common people of Cusco.

Atahualpa now found himself supreme ruler of Tahuantinsuyo, the empire weakened by civil war and disease, but with no power to match it in the known world. While he was celebrating his victory, about to make the long journey to Cusco to assume the throne, news reached him of the bearded, pale-skinned men who had landed on the northern coast near Tumbez. He decided to wait to see what the foreigners, maybe emissaries from the Creator-God Viracocha, would do next.

The Sacred River

The Upper Vilcanota

Most visitors to Cusco who do not arrive by air travel on the train from Puno or Arequipa. After passing over the seemingly endless expanse of altiplano that rises up to the 14,000 foot pass of La Raya, the descent into the Vilcanota valley makes a striking contrast. Where the altiplano is flat, wide and thinly populated, the Vilcanota valley is green, fertile, and densely settled with apparently prosperous communities. The houses may be built of adobe, but the shining corrugated-iron roofs announce the arrival of the twentieth century.

The Vilcanota's source is at a remote lake below the peaks of the same name. Following the river's course, there are soon signs of the agricultural terraces – 'andenes' – which the Incas built in such profusion that the Andes mountains were named after them. Many of these have fallen into disuse and are collapsing under the heavy feet of cattle. The springs that once fed the irrigation systems are often dry, the protective sponge of natural forest long since gone. But other terraces have been maintained over the centuries, and, with their irrigation channels still flowing, produce rich crops as they did at the height of the Inca empire.

One such place is at Raqchi, in the heart of the upper Vilcanota valley. The approach to the village square gives a sweeping view to the left over a green bowl of cultivation, while a high wall of close-fitting polygonal stonework stands to the right. The small village church looks like one of the clay model churches sold at festivals, not quite real. Just east of the village, a many-mouthed Inca stone fountain gushes with water from an underground channel, spreading out to irrigate the terraces.

It is hard to believe that, five hundred years ago, this was a major centre of Inca civilization and religion. But behind the huts that make up modern Raqchi, the ancient temple wall and the circular columns that once supported its roof rise forty feet or more high. Behind the wall and south-west is a succession of six connected squares, each with six dwellings built around in the same style, making a line of construction about a quarter of a mile long. Further to the west is a huge complex of 200 identical circular buildings, arranged back-to-back in rows of ten. Each building has a narrow opening into a space some twenty feet across, illuminated by small, high windows, the walls rising as high as ten feet.

The fertile agricultural floor of the Sacred Valley, seen over a fortified tower at the end of the main ridge at Pisac.

These circular buildings almost certainly pre-date the Incas by hundreds of years. Not only were circular buildings a rarity in Inca times, but the dry-stone construction is more typical of the earlier regional cultures, either Tiwanaku or Wari. But it is certain that the Incas continued to use them, probably as storehouses. It was the Incas, too, that built the site up into one of their most important temples – the principal one to Viracocha, the Creator-God. According to local legend, this was to propitiate him after a devastating volcanic upheaval.

The worship of Viracocha, which probably began under the later Incas, marked a departure from the earlier, animistic worship of natural phenomena – the sun, moon, stars, rainbow, thunder and lightning. The god Viracocha was recognized as being the creator of all these, and thus superior to them. Some authorities claim that Viracocha, represented by an oval of gold, occupied the highest place even at Coricancha. But the worship of this invisible god was restricted to those of higher intellect, more given to reflection. There were many prayers to Viracocha, one of which extols: 'Creator of the world, maker of all men, Lord of all Lords, My eyes fail me for longing to see you, For the sole desire to know you.' Contrary to the later accusations of religious zealots from Spain, anxious to justify the Conquest, the religion of the later Incas was fundamentally monotheistic: the natural phenomena were revered not as gods in their own right, but as manifestations of divine energy.

Raqchi is linked to Cusco by road and rail. Checacupe, twelve miles towards Cusco along an (unpaved) road, has an enormous church which is worth a visit but is invariably shut, and the key holder hard to track down. Also of interest is the single-arched colonial bridge across the gorge. From Checacupe the sixty miles to Cusco are along a paved road. There are other colonial churches along the way, most notably those at Andahuaylillas and Huaro containing the magnificent murals which are described in Chapter 4.

Next along the valley are the linked sites of Rumicolca (Stone Shed) and Pikillacta (Place of the Flea). The massive construction at Rumicolca is visible from the road. Near here the river Huatanay, which flows through Cusco twenty miles upstream, joins the Vilcanota. Pikillacta's extensive ruins lie just along the hillside from Rumicolca on the other side of the road. They were abandoned long before Inca domination of the region, probably as a result of water shortages. At the entrance to the site is

Above, the walls of the Temple of Viracocha, the creator god, at Ragchi. The lower part of the wall is of typical Inca cut and fitted masonry, while above it is of adobe. The roof tiles are a recent addition, to protect the adobe from rain.

Below, the huge stone gateway to the valley of Cusco at Rumicolca. The well-worked Inca stone around the double openings is an indication of its importance, probably to control access to the valley behind. But the Inca stonework is an overlay on a much older structure: originally the gateway supported an aqueduct which carried water to the Wari city of Pikillacta, just over the valley, and the water channels are still in evidence. The cruder masonry to the side of the double gates is of pre-Inca origin.

Above, view of the site of Pikillacta. The rough unworked stone is a striking contrast with the cut and fitted masonry of Inca sites. Interestingly, none of the buildings has doorways: as a defensive measure, all the entrances and other openings were on the first storey.

Below, detail of the irrigation system at Tipón, with water falling into a ritual bath and down into a water channel which feeds the terraces.

a large rectangular open space, built around with a high wall of unworked dry stone, still some twenty feet high in places, a remarkable feat for this type of construction. Some well-preserved agricultural terraces step up the hillside to the east. Clearly, neither terraces nor their irrigation systems were Inca inventions. The best view of the site is from the hillock to its north. From here the main part of the city on the higher ground behind the terraces can all be seen. Although the ruins are extensive, they are heavily overgrown and there is little of note to attract the inexperienced eye.

North-west of Pikillacta is a quarry which provided stone for the construction of Inca Cusco, for the Cathedral and other colonial buildings, and remains in continuous use to this day. The precise way in which the Incas cut out stones is not known. Probably the quarry men would enlarge fissures in the rock with wooden wedges, hammered in when dry, which would then expand when wetted. Additional wedges could then be inserted more deeply, and the process continued until the rock split. Once detached, the stone could be worked with stone hammers and axes, hand-held stones and brass chisels, while rollers and levers of wood and bronze were available to help move it. It seems that stones were worked roughly to shape at the quarry, leaving convenient protrusions, still visible on some large stones, with which to grip them. The stones would then be precisely cut and fitted on site.

The ruins of Choquepujío, sign-posted from the road, are a few miles past Pikillacta and ten minutes walk along the Huatanay. The overgrown site is on top of a small hill, and cattle graze around its plazas, watched by children. Although also Wari, the construction of Choquepujío is quite unlike that of Pikillacta; here the walls are built of small stones held together with mortar, with upper parts of adobe. In the centre are the remains of a three-storey double wall with funerary niches on both sides, which still reaches a considerable height. This suggests that the site may have been a burial place for Pikillacta.

From Choquepujío, the Vilcanota flows on down to Pisac and the Sacred Valley, while the road passes the gateway of Rumicolca to turn up the Huatanay valley towards Cusco. About five miles along, past the turning to Oropesa, and about fifteen miles outside Cusco, is a sign pointing to the little visited archaeological site of Tipón. The site itself is on the far side of the village, about an hour's walk or a bumpy car ride up the side of the valley.

Tipón is unforgettably lovely. It consists of a complex of agricultural terraces built up a narrow side valley, complete with their irrigation systems in full working order. At the top of the site a stone fountain is fed by a natural spring, still gushing out clear, cold water from the mountainside. The water is carried through intact irrigation channels, swimming with small frogs and fish, to the terraces, some of which are still producing healthy harvests of corn and potatoes. The mysterious remains of stone structures by the fountain may have been a water temple; even now, it is a tranquil place. A path leads further up the hillside to another sector of ruins with a large stone reservoir, used to feed the irrigation system below, and a temple of rough construction surrounding a huaca. The aqueduct to the reservoir can be followed higher still to a region of unexcavated terraces and buildings. A full day is needed to make the complete journey.

The stonework at Tipón is of high quality, especially in the lower region, indicating that the terraces were not intended for routine agriculture, but had some special purpose – possibly producing food for sacrifices, or for the Inca himself. It may be that the irrigated lower terraces with their milder climate were used for growing seedlings, which were then planted out in the upper zone when conditions permitted.

Every rainy season the rivers of the Andes run red, as more hillsides are stripped bare of their soil to reveal the bedrock below. But the Incas perfected agricultural techniques which allow the same land to produce rich harvests for hundreds of years without diminishing. One day agricultural experts may turn to places like Tipón so they can learn the techniques of five centuries ago and use them for the benefit of impoverished Andean communities.

The Sacred Valley

The next major site along the Vilcanota is at Pisac, at the head of the Sacred Valley (the popular name for the valley between Pisac and Ollantaytambo). Most visitors from Cusco take the road that skirts Sacsayhuaman, Puca Pucara and Tambo Machay before descending to the village of Pisac on the banks of the Vilcanota. From the road there are magnificent views of the valley. Pisac itself is a pretty market village with ancient 'pisonay' trees still gracing its square – a common species in the forests that once covered the surroundings.

The Pisaca sector of Pisac, seen from the ridge which runs down from Callacasa. The buildings are thought to have been home to the city's resident priests and nobles. The sector has been extensively restored and rebuilt — much of the work is archæologically suspect.

Above left, detail of the terracing below Callacasa, the upper complex at Pisac. The steps indicate that the terraces were used for agriculture and that any defensive purpose was secondary.

Above right, ritual bath in the temple complex around the Intihuatana at Pisac. It was probably used for ceremonial cleansing of priests before they carried out important rites.

Below, the Intihuatana (Hitching Post of the Sun) at Pisac. The quality of the stonework of the circular walls around the rock suggests that this was the most sacred spot in the city. The actual Intihuatana has been damaged, either by Spanish 'extirpators of idolatry' or by more recent vandals. Originally, it would have had a superstructure of precious metals and have been used for astronomical measurements.

Pisac's fame lies in the ruins that cover the crags towering over the village. Like so many Inca sites, Pisac was at different stages a fortress, an agricultural complex, and a centre for religion and administration. It was certainly a powerful fortress for a long time, occupying a strategic position between the western pass to Cusco and the eastern pass to Paucartambo, an Inca settlement in the fringes of the jungle. But the first impression of the site is of the terraces which step over 1,000 feet up the mountainside, and which must have made it a centre of abundant crop production.

Of course, the terraces would also have provided an effective defensive barrier against potential invaders, but at the height of the Inca empire there was no conceivable external threat. The jungle tribes of the Amazon, the 'Antis', did occasionally raid the eastern outposts of Tahuantinsuyo, but they were never a serious problem. They were interested in loot, not invasion, and had no desire to live in the dry, cold climate of the highlands. And if Pisac was such a great fortress in later years, it is odd that the Incas made no attempt to defend it during the Conquest, and that Manco Inca made no use of it during his rebellion.

There are two ways of arriving at the ruins: by the road that winds up the mountain to the north-east end of the site, or by foot on the steep path that leads from the main square of Pisac village, passing through the lower terraces. The best way to visit the ruins is to go straight to the group of buildings known as Callacasa at the top of the spur which dominates the site. The stonework here is coarse, probably much older than most of the other structures at Pisac. It can be difficult to find a way into the buildings, a good sign of defensive design, and Callacasa gives an aerial view of the site and of the valley below. Out along the line of the ridge, the precipices to the right fall away to the Quitamayo stream; just on the other side are a great many Inca tombs cut into the cliff face – they have all been raided by grave robbers, risking their lives in the process. The small complex of Canchisracay, at the end of the road to the site, lies far over to the left, while just to the left of the ridge is the semicircle of buildings known as Pisaca. In the valley below, the Vilcanota has an unusually straight course – this is one of the earliest canals in the Americas, built to maximize the area of cultivable land.

The most dramatic way down from here is to follow the well-built, but dizzying, Inca path down the ridge. In places, where the cliffs on each side are sheer, the path

Recreation of the original thatched roofing of houses in the lowest sector of Pisac, Corihuayrachina, below the Intihuatana on the path to the valley.

dives through tunnels hollowed into the rock. About fifteen minutes away, the main temple complex is instantly recognizable by its remarkably fine rectangular masonry, some of the best in existence. At the centre of the area is a large rock built around with coursed stone, with its apex carved into an Intihuatana. The purpose of the other buildings is unknown, but they are thought to include a Temple of the Moon and a shrine to Viracocha, and perhaps a lodge for the Inca. The bath at the lower end of the complex, with its water supply carved across a cliff face, may have been used for ritual purposes. Pisac is a large site, measuring about a mile from north to south. It needs at least half a day to explore; failing that, a couple of hours are needed even for a rapid scout around.

Calca, the present administrative centre of the Sacred Valley about ten miles down from Pisac, is the starting-point for the ruins of Huchuy Cosco (Little Cusco), which are some of the least visited in the valley, and in an unusually good state of preservation. They are high in the mountains to the south, overlooking Calca several thousand feet below. The walk requires either a guide or detailed instructions, and an early departure is recommended to avoid the sun while climbing. Most of the path follows a steep Inca stone road, now almost completely destroyed by cattle; before the Conquest, the only traffic consisted of people and light-footed llamas; many an Inca road has now been damaged beyond recognition by the horses and cattle that came with the conquistadors. Once, the mountain was covered in rich green forest, but this has been burnt off for pasture, a few tufts of grass poking out of the bare earth between the cacti and coarse shrubs.

The main arena of Huchuy Cosco, running along an east-west axis, is the size of a football field. As the only flat ground for miles around, it is used for that purpose – there are goalposts at either end. To the west is a large square building two storeys high, its otherwise perfect stonework split by a crack from a long past earthquake. A little beyond is a large stone-sided sunken enclosure that looks like a swimming pool – although this interpretation seems unlikely, and the water supply has yet to be discovered, no one has yet come up with a better explanation.

Just above the high wall to the south of the arena is a 'kallanka', a long building with open doorways, used to house passing travellers. Further back another building houses a huge unworked boulder of unknown significance. The building is of the

same high-quality masonry evident throughout the site, complete with trapezoidal niches. These still retain their smooth facing of hard mud plaster, except where it has been gouged out to display the logo of a vandalistic Peruvian travel company.

The next major town down the valley from Calca is Urubamba, undistinguished both in history and in archaeology. But shortly before Urubamba is the pretty village of Yucay, generally ignored by tour operators. It has two large grassy squares with huge pisonay trees; one of the squares contains the post-Conquest remains of Inca Sayri Tupac's palace, built largely of adobe in a style recognizably different from classic Inca. Sayri Tupac was Manco Inca's son, born in 1535 in the independent state of Vilcabamba, and became Inca at the age of five following his father's death. Sayri Tupac was tempted from Vilcabamba by the Spanish and was granted estates near Yucay, where he built his palace; to the chagrin of the Spanish, his brother Titu Cusi took his place in Vilcabamba. Sayri Tupac was a model puppet Inca, even converting to Christianity, until his suspicious death at the age of twenty-five. Up behind the village are extensive agricultural terraces, fed with water from the snow caps and glaciers above.

One of the most unusual sights of the valley is Las Salinas, the salt pans, between Urubamba and Ollantaytambo up a side valley to the south-west. They are just visible from the road, sparkling white in the sunshine across an entire hillside a few miles away. It is quite easy to visit them, across a footbridge at Tarabamba and a mile down the river, before turning up the steep side valley. The path is usually busy with old women, donkeys and sometimes whole families groaning their way down under the weight of sacks of salt. It is best to arrive in the morning, when the pans are in sunshine.

The salt pans exist because the rocks of the area have a very high salt content, which is slowly leached out by rainwater. A more dramatic manifestation of this is at the Inca agricultural centre at Moray, which can be reached either on foot continuing up the valley from Las Salinas, or by track from the town of Maras (often impassable to vehicles). By either route, it is best to recruit the services of a local guide, and allow the best part of a day for the trip.

At Moray the leaching out of salt over a long period of time, and consequent subsidence, has led to the formation of four large craters measuring up to half a mile across the top and over a hundred feet deep. At some unknown time, probably before the Incas, an interesting discovery was made: that the climate at the bottom of the craters is quite different from that at the top, with temperatures dropping rapidly towards the lower levels. This made the craters an ideal environment for developing and testing new crop strains. The concentric circles of terraces around the craters, which survive to this day, are largely of Inca stonework, with some apparently pre-Inca elements. The effect of the terraces was to accentuate the natural temperature difference between the levels. In modern terms, Moray was an agricultural research station in which each terrace simulated the climate of a different altitude. Local people call Moray the 'greenhouse of the Incas', as good a description as any.

This may seem an unlikely theory, but the Inca empire depended on a well-fed population producing surpluses of food to support its armies, labourers, administrators, priesthood and nobility, and for sacrifices. So it is hardly surprising that they would work on the development of new crop strains, allowing, for example, maize and the proteinous Andean grain of quinoa to be grown at higher altitudes than previously. An important aspect of Inca colonization in higher regions was the introduction of high-altitude varieties of maize where potatoes had previously been the staple crop. This was preferable to the Incas, as the maize was more easily transported and stored, and formed the basis of their favourite drink, chicha. Moray may well have been where those crop strains were developed for use throughout the empire.

The village of Chinchero lies on a tributary of the Urubamba. It can be reached either by foot on an Inca road that rises out of the Sacred Valley, or along the paved road to Cusco that climbs up an alarmingly eroded mountainside, before reaching flatter, more stable land above. Soon passing the turn-off to Maras and Moray, the road winds on to Chinchero, now an impoverished community which survives on tourism and its Sunday market as necessary additions to subsistence agriculture.

The scale of the ruins indicates that Chinchero was a very different place in Inca times. Much of the village is built on original Inca walls, while extensive terraces sweep out into the valley below. Chinchero was the Inca administrative centre for this whole high, windswept region, before which it may well have been the capital

Above, the salt-pans at Las Salinas. They have been in use since Inca times, and the salt extraction technology has remained unchanged. The system of family and community rights to individual salt pans has probably stayed the same, too, in spite of the salt boom under the Spanish, who needed huge amounts for the extraction of silver from ore.

Below, the largest of the four craters at Moray. The terracing is largely of Inca origin, with some apparently earlier elements. The terraces were restored a few years ago, but are now neglected and are crumbling under the feet of the sheep and goats put out to graze there.

Above left, an original Inca doorway, now at the foot of the church bell-tower at Chinchero.

Above right, woman selling coca leaves in the market at Chinchero – now as in Inca times, the leaves are sacred, and the coca trade is an important part of the local economy. Only the respected elder women of a village may sell them. In the colonial era, the Spanish made great use of coca to make the most of indigenous forced labour. Now of course, the cocaine trade dominates the rural economy in many areas of Peru, bringing the private armies and violence that disrupt the lives of ordinary peasant communities.

Below, local women on market day at Chinchero. The Inca wall behind is part of the original temple enclosure now used as the village square.

of a small independent state. Its importance at the time of the Conquest is also indicated by the size of its now rather decayed church.

Chinchero is one of several places in this book described as administrative centres, a term which needs further explanation. The Inca empire, as we have seen, depended on large surpluses of food and manpower, ultimately provided by tributes from the toiling Inca peasantry. They were raised in two ways: first, every landholding was divided into three parts, only one of which was for the sustenance of its farmers – the produce of the other two parts was destined for the Inca; and second, each able-bodied man was required to spend a part of the year working for the Inca, under the 'mita' system that was to be so severely abused by the Spanish. To raise this tribute fairly and without error required accurate information about every subject and the crops and land of every community. The Inca administrators acquired and maintained this information, even sending summaries back for the imperial records in Cusco; and they made sure that the tributes were received. All the many centres were linked together by highways with relays of messengers carrying information backwards and forwards at great speed. In short, Tahuantin-suyo was a humming hive of efficient administration.

The Incas achieved this remarkable efficiency without the aid of writing. Messages were transmitted orally, with the help of a complex mnemonic system of multi-coloured knotted strings known as 'quipus', which were also used to record accounts and statistics, as well as other less tangible information. But quipus were so difficult to use that a special class of people, the 'quipamayocs', spent years learning to tie and interpret them; and even they usually needed an oral message to understand a new quipu.

Ollantaytambo

Ollantaytambo is both the last and the single most important site in the Sacred Valley, both for its architecture and its history. Strategically located above a narrow stretch of the Urubamba river (the former Vilcanota), on the border between the highlands and the lower jungle valleys, it guards important valleys on either side of the river. Like Pisac, Ollantaytambo was a major centre of religion, agriculture and administration. Unlike Pisac, we know that it was used as a fort and was twice proved invincible by direct assault.

Ollantaytambo receives its name from events that took place during Pachacutec's reign, when Ollanta, the viceroy of Antisuyo, and the Inca's daughter, Cusi Coyllar (Joyful Star), fell in love. Pachacutec swiftly imprisoned Cusi Coyllar and her love child, forcing Ollanta into rebellion. Ollanta recruited an army of Antis and took control of the fortress, which he held against the Inca's armies. After the ageing Inca's death and Tupac Yupanqui's accession, Ollanta was deceived into letting down his defences, and the fortress was taken by the Inca's soldiers. But Tupac Yupanqui relented, reunited the loving couple, and reinstated Ollanta as viceroy of Antisuyo. Ever since, the fortress has carried his name, and this romantic tale is handed down in one of a small number of extant Inca dramas.

Certainly, the main ruins at Ollantaytambo occupy a highly defensible position on a craggy spur of rock that juts out into the fertile valley. The view of the rows of terraces, seventeen in all, that rise up steeply from the village square to the main buildings is daunting enough for most visitors, even without fierce Inca warriors to defend them. The terracing served a dual purpose as fortification and as a source of food for sacrificial offerings. There is a number of ruined structures at the foot of the terraces, including the Baño de la Ñusta (Maiden's Bath), famous for its harmonious design. A stone stairway goes from here up to the temple complex.

The most striking feature of the temple buildings is the six enormous stones, each about nine feet high and more than fifty tons in weight, separated by stone spacers a few inches wide. It is hard to imagine how they were transported from the quarry at Caticancha over three miles away on the other side of the river. The temple was apparently still under construction at the time of the Conquest, as not only are there stones on site that have still not been placed in position, but there is a long train of stones abandoned between the quarry and Ollantaytambo.

The buildings behind the temple include storehouses, long buildings with pitched roofs. To the west of the temple area, where the slopes are more gradual, a massive defensive wall rises up to a height of about fifteen feet. Maybe it was also intended to break the force of the wind and trap the heat of the sun, creating a benign microclimate in the temple and the terraces below. A path leads through an opening in the wall and up the hillside to an isolated building with some mysterious man-sized

The town of Ollantaytambo and the Sacred Valley, seen from the ruins above. At the foot of the picture is the recently excavated area including the Baño de la Ñusta.

Above, Chinchero's large but now decaying church shows the town's greater importance at the time of the Conquest. The wall beneath, with its twelve niches, was part of a major temple – the upper part was dismantled to build the church.

Below, the Baño de la Ñusta at Ollantaytambo, on the valley floor to the right of the entrance. The name is a recent invention, but certainly this was a ceremonial bathing place, probably part of a water temple. This sector was excavated in the late 'seventies, revealing a larger complex of buildings, water channels and temple enclosures than previously suspected.

niches and a commanding view over the valley to both sides. One theory is that the niches were used to tie up prisoners; the holes in the jambs would certainly make this possible.

This is a good place from which to see the 'Avenue of the Hundred Niches' in the valley below, actually a road passing through a huge Inca building of which just a single wall, complete with niches, remains. The trapezoidal street plan of the village, unchanged since the Conquest, is also clearly laid out below, and provides a good example of Inca town planning. The Inca names of the blocks are used to this day, and the original Inca houses are still inhabited. Also present are the adobe brick factories, mining the alluvial soil to provide materials for Cusco's construction boom. A walk up behind the village clearly demonstrates the importance of Ollantaytambo as an agricultural centre, for the valley contains one of the most extensive surviving systems of irrigated agricultural terraces.

Further up the valley are the fascinating pre-Inca ruins of Pumamarca, about two hours walk away. The path follows the Patacancha stream from the village square along its right bank, and crosses a bridge to enter a region of wide Inca terraces, over a hundred yards across, whose rich crops support a prosperous community. At the village of Huiñaypata the path to Pumamarca forks off to the left, following an Inca wall, and rises through a further immense system of terraces, partly defaced by eucalyptus plantations, that continues for several miles along the left side of the valley. Many of the irrigation channels are in perfect condition but mostly disused, as their springs have run dry as a result of the destruction of the cloud forest above. The Incas knew that the fertility of their land was intimately connected with the health and vigour of the surrounding natural vegetation and protected their forests, but deforestation was well under way within years of the Conquest, and has continued ever since.

The red-stoned ruins of Pumamarca are soon visible ahead, prominent on a mountain spur. The layout of the site leaves no doubt that it was a fort, surrounded as it is by high defensive walls. The crude dry stonework is pre-Inca, but some adobe buildings are still in a surprisingly good state of preservation, complete with wooden lintels over trapezoidal doors and windows. These must be Inca additions, as little

One of the enormous blocks of pink granite near the main temple complex at Ollantaytambo. This area was apparently unfinished at the time of the Conquest, as not only are there such blocks on the site that were never finally positioned, but there is also a long train of abandoned stones between the quarry and Ollantaytambo.

Above, detail of the stonework of the main temple at Ollantaytambo. It is often called the Temple of the Sun, but there is no evidence to support the name. The thin stone spacers between the main blocks, and the geometric relief pattern, are unique in known Inca ruins. There is a number of theories about the design, none convincing.

Below left, inside the main temple enclosure at Pumamarca. The niches were probably used for storing mummies. The stonework is clearly pre-Inca, but archaeological finds at the site indicate that it was in use in Inca times.

Below right, storehouses high on the other side of the valley to Ollantaytambo. They were probably used to store perishable food stuffs, as the position benefits from cooling breezes. Such storehouses were a common feature of the Inca landscape, and were used to store supplies and agricultural surpluses: corn, chuna (freeze-dried potato), quinoa, woollen shoes, blankets, coca leaves, weapons, and even the iridescent feathers used for ceremonial dress. The stores were kept permanently stocked, ready for times of famine or shortage, or for the passage of an Inca army. Although stocks were low at the time of the Conquest as a result of the civil war, the Spanish were greatly impressed. Predictably, the storehouses were plundered during the Conquest, and the ordinary people of Peru have never again enjoyed the same security against crop failure or natural disaster.

wood has survived so well from pre-Inca times – perhaps, while at Ollantaytambo, Manco Inca renovated the fort as a possible place of retreat. The site is divided into two parts, the lower walled part and a small undefended part some fifty yards up the ridge.

The second time that Ollantaytambo is known to have been used as a fortress was after the Conquest, during Manco Inca's Great Rebellion. After abandoning his base at Calca, he decided upon Ollantaytambo as a more defensible stronghold. Hernando Pizarro led a force of his best men down the Sacred Valley with the intention of capturing or killing the rebel Inca, but was appalled at the resistance he met. Every terrace was filled with warriors, including archers from the jungle tribes, and slingers and soldiers armed with captured Spanish weapons. As the Spanish retreated under the hail of stones, rocks and arrows, Manco's men attacked 'with such a tremendous shout it seemed as if the mountain was crashing down', then diverted the river Patacancha (which runs through the village square) to flood the field of battle, immobilizing Pizarro's dreaded cavalry. The Spanish promptly retreated. By the time they returned, Manco Inca had left, to seek a safer refuge deep in the jungles of the Cordillera Vilcabamba.

When Francisco Pizarro took the Inca Atahualpa captive in the famous attack at Cajamarca, it was as if a chess grandmaster had been checkmated at first move. Even after the ravages of the civil war, the empire had ample resources which could have been mobilized to destroy the conquistadors; but by capturing the Inca, who continued to rule while their prisoner, the Spanish commandeered those resources to do their own work. This work was the looting of the treasures of Tahuantinsuyo, the enslavement of its people and the destruction of its social order, to be replaced with alien Spanish ways. Had Atahualpa known this, he might not have been so co-operative.

But throughout the history of the Conquest one theme emerges: that the Incas failed to understand the enormity of what was happening until too late. Atahualpa was looking forward to his release once the ransom of a roomful of gold had been paid. Only when the Spanish had been given licence to strip the holiest of Cusco's temples, and the ransom had been paid in full, did he suspect the truth. He died miserably, sentenced by a kangaroo court with Francisco Pizarro as judge. The only mercy shown was that he was strangled rather than burnt, thanks to his last minute conversion to Christianity. Given Atahualpa's crimes, maybe he deserved no better, but the same cannot be said of his subjects, who were left to face a new system of institutionalized exploitation and oppression.

The first Spaniards to enter Cusco received an extraordinary welcome, though they came only to plunder. In the words of a 1685 translation of the chronicler Garcilaso de la Vega:

> The people coming forth to meet them received them with great joy and mirth, with music and dances . . . nor were the Spaniards less surprised to see the majesty of Cusco, with the grandeur and riches of the palaces . . . the gentle behaviour of the nobles, and the courtesy of the commonality, who were all desirous to serve them and gain their favour.

Of course the invaders came with the authority of the captive Inca, but their popularity is perhaps better explained by the fact that Atahualpa was himself considered a usurper. His massacre of Huascar's family and supporters, amounting to several hundred of Cusco's royalty and nobility, made him many enemies. Although Atahualpa's prisoner, the deposed Huascar, was at least alive, and the

The classic view of Machu Picchu, the whole city seen from the upper part of the agricultural terracing to its south, with the peak of Huayna Picchu (Young Mountain) behind. The path up to the summit can just be made out.

Spanish were widely seen as liberators sent by the gods to restore him. To quote José de la Riva Aguero, the empire was 'rent by a devastating, sacriligious civil war started by Atahualpa, a land morally depressed and exhausted ... The Inca ruling class had no choice but to receive as help sent from heaven those who, to all appearances, had come to avenge them and save them from extermination.'

Francisco Pizarro understood and exploited Tahuantinsuyo's internal divisions. He was furious when Huascar was murdered, apparently on Atahualpa's orders, as it limited his scope for playing the two sides off against each other. So when Manco Inca, a former supporter of his brother Huascar, came to greet Pizarro as Cusco's liberator, he was well received. Manco was one of two surviving sons of Huayna Capac, and immensely popular with the native population – in short, the perfect puppet Inca. He was soon enthroned with great scenes of rejoicing from both Indians and Spanish. From that time on, Cusco was firmly allied with the Spanish against the forces left by Atahualpa, which continued to put up a powerful opposition.

It took Manco Inca several years of abuse and humiliation before he realized the true nature of the Spanish presence. By then the great Inca armies were sadly weakened, but this did not prevent him from launching the Great Rebellion against the Spanish for which he mobilized over 100,000 men. Although the Spanish were weakened by internal strife between Diego de Almagro and the Pizarros, the rebellion ended in failure. It was only through sheer luck that Manco Inca and a band of followers escaped. An expedition followed Manco as far as Vitcos, at the head of the Vilcabamba valley, but was distracted by a golden Punchao and other valuables in the temple, complete with Sun Virgins. While the soldiers were busy with these unexpected finds, Manco Inca disappeared over the mountains to a more inaccessible region. Here, in the place known as Vilcabamba, he founded an independent kingdom from which to resist Spanish rule.

In little over five years, the vast Inca empire had been reduced to a remote jungle stronghold. Its treasures had been looted and sent to Spain. Its population had been halved by war, disease and famine, their herds of llamas slaughtered, and even their seed corn exacted as tribute. The tribute paid to the new masters was greater than before, though the people were fewer in number – and none of the tribute was used for public works or stores, but all for Spanish profit. The temples had been desecrated

The final stairs of the Inca path up Huayna Picchu.

The south-eastern corner of the city of Machu Picchu, seen from near the modern entrance, in the agricultural sector. This group of houses includes the Condor Temple, and is sometimes known as the Aristocratic Quarter, as the standard of construction is higher than that of the adjacent Industrial Sector.

and zealous Christian priests were travelling the country punishing any who continued to practice the old religion. The Inca systems of administration were abandoned, or perverted to serve the purposes of the new regime.

For many, Manco Inca represented the only hope for the future, and this made his destruction a first priority for the Spanish. To add urgency, Manco's warriors were terrorizing Spanish merchants on the royal highway between Lima and Cusco, and other native armies were causing havoc in the northern highlands and south beyond lake Titicaca. But one by one, the rebellions were put down, with reprisals to discourage others. In one pacification exercise which followed the killing of two Spanish tribute collectors, 600 children under the age of three alone were put to death.

After Manco was forced back to Vilcabamba by Francisco Pizarro in early 1539, a Spanish army set off after him. Despite ambushes and Vilcabamba's natural defences, which caused the expedition both hardship and casualties, Manco's capital was burnt to the ground, and his sister-wife Cura Occlo captured. But once again, Manco Inca took to the hills. The next step for the Spanish was to send envoys to him. When they were returned decapitated, Francisco Pizarro in his fury executed all the captured native commanders, had Cura Ocllo shot full of arrows and floated her body down the Urubamba. Manco returned to reconstruct Vilcabamba, where he remained for five years until murdered at Vitcos by Spanish outlaws who had taken refuge with him, and who hoped in this way to regain favour in Cusco.

It was not until 1572 that a Spanish army was to return to Vilcabamba. A number of envoys had been there in intervening years, first to negotiate for Manco's successor, Inca Sayri Tupac, to return to Cusco. After Sayri Tupac's departure, his brother Titu Cusi took over. He maintained Inca traditions and ceremonies, and kept a huge golden Punchao which was much venerated. His negotiations with the Spanish were protracted if inconclusive, and this probably helped keep them at bay. But the scene rapidly changed after Titu Cusi's death in 1571 and the accession of Tupac Amaru, which coincided with the arrival of the new Viceroy, de Toledo, who soon sent a powerful expedition finally to destroy this intolerable affront to Spanish rule.

The expedition encountered little resistance, reaching Vilcabamba almost without

Machu Picchu seen from the peak of Huayna Picchu. The curving road up from the railway station is named in honour of Hiram Bingham. Locals claim that the curves look like pregnant women. Unlike the better known views, this shows clearly the division of Machu Picchu into the agricultural sector and the actual ceremonial centre.

The Watchman's Hut at Machu Picchu, probably a look-out or communications post, standing at the top of the agricultural terraces.

casualties, only to find it abandoned and burnt to the ground: once again, the Inca had fled. But Tupac Amaru faced determined adversaries, who pursued him deep into the forest; here, with the help of captured Indians, the Inca and his wife were found. After being assured that they would come to no harm, they surrendered and were taken back to Cusco. Tupac Amaru was the second Inca to die following a sham trial, and his death sentence was much lamented in Cusco. Not only was he innocent of any crime, he was also, in the words of one chronicler, 'affable, well-disposed and discreet, eloquent and intelligent'; he presented no threat to Spanish rule, and was for many the symbol of a past age of romance and mystery. His summary execution in the Plaza de Armas marked the end of an era.

The search for Vilcabamba

After Tupac Amaru's death, the city of Vilcabamba was forgotten and the surrounding forests soon reclaimed the abandoned fields and buildings. The only records of the city were in the writings of chroniclers, but they were not concerned with conveying accurate directions. It was not until the early nineteenth century that interest revived in Vilcabamba, and then from abroad. The first expeditions focused on Choquequirau, a late Inca site magnificently located on a forested mountain spur some 5,000 feet above the Apurímac canyon, on the fringes of the Cordillera Vilcabamba. Among its visitors, in early 1909, was a young American archaeologist from Yale called Hiram Bingham.

Although Bingham did not believe the claims made of Choquequirau, he was inspired by what he saw: the views over the steep, forested mountains; and the ruins of lost cities, hidden under the dark tangle of tropical vegetation. His next expedition left Cusco in mid 1911. A few days journey down the Urubamba valley, a peasant came to investigate the unusual-looking party and mentioned the existence of some ruins in the hills across the river. Bingham left early the next morning to investigate, and on a wide platform between two mountains, covered with thick forest, he found a group of ruins the size of a small city and with classic Inca masonry. These ruins, to be the most famous in the Americas, took the name of the peak that rises above the site to the south – Machu Picchu (Old Mountain).

Bingham carried on down the Urubamba and then turned up the Vilcabamba

Above, the Funerary Rock at Machu Picchu, carved in situ *on the south side of the graveyard zone near the Watchman's Hut. It is thought to have been used for the laying out and mummification of bodies.*

Below left, the Intihuatana (Hitching Post of the Sun) at Machu Picchu. Major Inca sites invariably have one, but this example is uniquely well preserved, as Spanish 'extirpators of idolatry' were zealous in disfiguring all those they could find.

Below right, a small enclosure carved out of the living rock, beneath Machu Picchu's Industrial Sector to its west. Its purpose is not known, but it forms part of the area sometimes known as the Lower Graveyard. Like the Funerary Rock at the main graveyard, it may have been used for the laying out and embalming of bodies.

Left, the Industrial Sector, seen from the Temple of the Three Windows, on the other side of the main plaza.

Above, the original main gate to Machu Picchu, seen from inside the enclosure, with the agricultural terracing rising up behind. The gate was of wood, and the holes in the wall would have been used to hang it and, when necessary, to tie it securely shut.

valley. First he was taken by local people to ruins high on the forested ridge of Rosaspata. There was one huge building, nearly 250 feet long, and another fourteen smaller buildings around a large square; the masonry was excellent, an indication of a royal palace or ceremonial site. All the evidence suggested that these were the ruins of Vitcos, where Manco Inca was murdered by his Spanish guests. To confirm his discovery, Bingham began to search for the Temple of the Sun, the 'centre of idolatry in the latter part of the Inca rule', as described by chroniclers. He soon found it, a huge white granite monolith standing above a dark pool, all surrounded by the remains of a temple. As at Quenqo, seats have been carved into the monolith, and elaborate channels cut for sacrificial blood and chicha.

Bingham carried on, eventually reaching Espíritu Pampa (Plain of the Spirits) in the hot lowland valley of Pampaconas. There he came across the extensive remains of an Inca city hidden beneath buttress-rooted trees and tangled lianas. But Bingham only explored an outer corner of the site, and failed to realize the extent of the ruins. He did notice some red roofing tiles, whose use was introduced by the Spanish, putting the date of the site firmly after the Conquest. But the expedition was growing restless and Bingham was anxious to find out how the site clearance at Machu Picchu was proceeding. Bingham's departure from Espíritu Pampa marked the end of an extraordinary month in the history of archaeology.

Machu Picchu

Visitors to Machu Picchu today have a very different experience from Hiram Bingham in 1911. A 3 foot gauge railway line leads from Cusco down the Urubamba valley, with a station below Machu Picchu. From the station, a road cuts up the mountain, and minibuses ply the route. At the top of the road, a hotel and other modern buildings are unavoidably prosaic. The site has been thoroughly cleared, and short grass has replaced the tangle of trees. This makes it possible to climb up to one of several vantage points and see what Bingham could not until years of clearance and excavation had passed – the ruins spread out with map-like clarity.

With the benefit of new historical and archaeological knowledge, several long-held assumptions can be reversed. For example, it had been thought that Machu Picchu was an exclusively Inca site; but in late 1988 Carbon-14 tests indicated that the site was settled as early as AD 800, six hundred years before the Inca empire reached here. One burial has been dated back some 2,000 years. Another long-held belief was that Machu Picchu was an isolated centre, surrounded by nothing but forest. In fact, the entire area is rich in ruins, all interconnected by stone pathways; new discoveries are made whenever finances permit exploration. Most recently a huge stone staircase has been discovered that climbs several thousand feet up the moutain across the Urubamba valley, and many temples and ceremonial terraces have been found on the lower slopes of Huayna Picchu, the mountain to the north of the site. These have been left to the jungle, as there are no funds for their upkeep.

More importantly, Bingham and many others were convinced that Machu Picchu was Manco Inca's capital, Vilcabamba. It was not until Gene Savoy, another American archaeologist, made his expedition to Espíritu Pampa in 1964 that the truth was established – that Bingham had failed to recognize the ruins for what they were. Savoy uncovered the full extent of the site, the main part of which began a quarter of a mile from Bingham's excavations, with buildings stretching half a mile from end to end. Corroborative evidence was provided by various chronicles and letters, many of them unknown to Bingham. The solution to the mystery of Vilcabamba created a deeper one around Machu Picchu.

Machu Picchu was certainly a major Inca centre, not only for its rich subtropical agriculture, but also as a royal residence and ceremonial complex. The natural location, the density of temples and the quality of construction leave no doubt. The architectural style is late imperial Inca, dating it to the last century of Inca rule. Apparently, Machu Picchu was one of a number of temple-palaces like Ollantay-tambo and Pisac, with the difference that the Spanish do not seem to have known about it, indicating that it was not in use at the time of the Conquest. Machu Picchu must have been abandoned before then: either it had been forgotten, or it was considered of no consequence.

In the wooded hillside on the far side of Huayna Picchu (Young Mountain), there is a recently excavated funerary cave-temple, with masonry and double arches of the very highest quality, indicating a royal tomb. Strangely, it was abandoned in mid-construction. One reason for this might be that the person for whom it was intended had died prematurely, and was buried elsewhere. Huayna Capac lived his

The south-eastern corner of Machu Picchu in the early morning mists, seen from near the modern entrance.

last years in Quito, in the north. He had long considered returning to Cusco, but had refrained as he did not like its cold, dry climate. One theory about Machu Picchu is that he built a city there for his return. It was already a major agricultural centre supplying Cusco, and had a suitably impressive location and a mild, wet climate. But Huayna Capac died in an epidemic before he could move south. In the mourning that followed, Machu Picchu, a place now sacred to him, was abandoned. The treasures were returned to Cusco, its priests and Sun Virgins went to other temples; and the workforce was soon conscripted into Huascar's army against Atahualpa. Thus, eight years before the Conquest, Machu Picchu was lost to the world.

Like all other theories about Machu Picchu, this is pure speculation, in this case by the authors. It is fairly certain that Pachacutec was the first Inca to develop the area, one of his first conquests. Beyond that, we simply do not know its history and purpose.

Most of the visitors to Machu Picchu arrive on the morning train and leave in the afternoon, allowing just four hours at the ruins, only enough for a quick exploration. Two full days can easily be spent exploring the ruins and other nearby places of interest. It is worth arriving early in the morning, when the ruins are relatively empty; from the settlement of Aguas Calientes, this involves a good half hour's climb up the steep footpath before the trains and buses arrive.

The main entrance now is at the lower south-east corner of the site, through a small residential area known as the Terrace Caretakers' Houses. These are on the edge of the agricultural terraces to the south of the main urban sector. Some of the houses have been restored, with steep thatched roofs tied back by leather straps. The houses are of simple construction; they were probably occupied by workers, too humble to sleep in the ceremonial centre.

To get the lie of the land, a good starting place is the Watchman's Hut, a vantage point with a view of the entire site. This is almost directly above the entrance, a small thatched building reached up the stairs on the far side of the first terraces. Behind the hut is an area where many human remains have been found, which was used as a graveyard. Along the terraces to the north west is the original main entrance to the site. Running straight down the slope from here is the dry ditch that separates the city centre from the agricultural terraces, with a long stone stairway up its side.

Ruins of a small complex near the peak of Huayna Picchu. It could have been a temple, a look-out point or a signalling post – probably all three.

Above, the temple enclosure of the Intihuatana, seen from the Sacred Plaza.

Below, the 'beak of the condor' at the Condor Temple. It is debatable whether the carving really is a condor – some archæologists think that it is a more abstract fertility symbol.

The city is divided into two main areas by a wide grassy esplanade, presumably the setting for religious and other gatherings. Most of the temples and religious or royal buildings, recognizable by their excellent stonework, are in the Religious Sector, to the west of the plaza (left, as seen from the Watchman's Hut). The main gateway leads to a group of houses of functional stonework, maybe for skilled workers, as ordinary workers would have lived in houses of adobe. An area of rocky outcrops used as a quarry is just to the west.

The group of more distinguished buildings to the east includes the Temple of the Sun, also known as The Tower, the only circular building at Machu Picchu. The temple is built on solid rock, and beneath it is a cave called The Inca's Tomb, used for the storage of mummies. North of the temple is a ceremonial area, with an intricate system of water channels and ritual baths, and across a stairway, the massively built Inca's Palace. The water that once ran to this area along an aqueduct is now piped into the Hotel. Other buildings in this group have, rather speculatively, been named the Fountain Caretaker's House and the Palace of the Princess.

Continuing north, and still to the west of the esplanade, are the buildings known as the Temple of the Three Windows, the Principal Temple and the Sacristy, built around a roughly square plaza. This complex features some of the most carefully worked Inca masonry found anywhere, and includes one stone in the doorway between the Principal Temple and the Sacristy which has a total of thirty-two corners. Linked to this complex is the temple of the Intihuatana, probably the most sacred place in all Machu Picchu. At the centre is the Intihuatana, a beautifully sculptured rock rising to a graceful pillar of grey granite a few feet high, used for measuring the movements of the sun, moon and stars.

Across the plaza are various sectors of more mundane buildings, including another group of ordinary houses, with the small Temple of the Moon on its north side towards Huayna Picchu. Further in the same direction is the 'Sacred Rock', a flat monolith standing on its side, whose outline matches that of the mountains behind. Back towards the modern entrance is the Industrial Sector, thought to have been occupied by craftsmen, or other of the more privileged workers. The masonry in these sectors is mostly of rough stone, except for the facing to the plaza. At the time of writing, the buildings in the lower eastern part of this area were undergoing complete demolition and rebuilding, an investment of limited resources which might be better made in the preservation of endangered sites elsewhere.

The final group of buildings, on the south-eastern corner of the city, includes the so-called Prison, more likely have been a temple. It is just possible to make out the outline of a condor carved on the floor of the Prison's underground chamber; for this reason, the building is also called the Temple of the Condor.

The peak that rises up to the north is Huayna Picchu, which has an Inca path cutting across its sheer cliffs to the summit. The climb is recommended only to those with a good head for heights, and with at least two hours to spare. A surprising discovery near the top is a series of narrow terraces, presumably ceremonial, as routine agriculture could never have been practical here. Another trail leads to the Temple of the Moon, overlooking the Urubamba on the other side of Huayna Picchu, but has now been closed off.

The walk up Machu Picchu itself is more difficult. It follows the Inca road that passes just east of and below the Watchman's Hut, past a region of large terraces, before turning right through the low, thorny scrub. An easier walk is to follow the stone road the two miles to Intipunktu (Gateway of the Sun). Intipunktu has some Inca buildings, but is worth visiting more for the splendid views of Machu Picchu. Further on down this path, about two hours from Machu Picchu, are the ruins of Huiñay Huayna, named after the 'Forever Young' orchid of the region (see p.87).

The Inca trail

> One of the things which most took my attention. . . was how the great and splendid highways that we see throughout it could be built. . . These highways were so long, one of them more than 1,100 leagues, over mountains so rough and dismaying that in certain places one could not see the bottom, and some of the slopes so sheer and barren that the road had to be cut through the hard rock to keep it level and the right width. . . there are no words to describe what they were like when we saw them. . .

These words were written by the chronicler Cieza de León, who arrived in Peru in time to witness to the wonders of Tahuantinsuyo. For those who want to experience what he was writing about at first hand, there is an alternative way of getting to

Machu Picchu. The 'Inca Trail' covers a three-day trek which begins a little way beyond Ollantaytambo at the stop known as Kilometre 88. Its name is misleading, as this is just one of many Inca trails leading across the Andes; but it is in a good state of repair, passes through varied climates and landscapes and leads to a number of beautiful ruins before reaching Machu Picchu.

The Inca Trail and most of its sites were originally discovered by Hiram Bingham in his 1915 expedition. Later, in 1940–1, a 900-strong expedition under Paul Fejos traced and cleared most of the trail, and discovered the ruins of Huiñay Huayna and Intipata (Hill of the Sun).

The first ruins are just above the Urubamba at Llactapata. A trapezoidal plaza is surrounded by buildings and courtyards, in turn surrounded by a whole hillside of irrigated terraces. The recently restored ruins of Pultipuyoc with its large circular tower around a sacred rock are a few hundred yards north-west. The terraces were recently the subject of the 'Cusichaca Project', which investigated the site and restored some of the irrigation systems. Many of the terraces here are believed to pre-date the Incas' presence by hundreds of years.

The Trail climbs steeply from here, with a detour off to the left to the ruined tambo (travellers' lodge) at Paucarcancha, on the Inca road from Cusco which passes the peak of Salcantay. Bounded on two sides by streams, it has a central bastion protected by two well-made walls, while seven levels of terraces rise up to a peak behind. The Trail itself continues westwards and passes through a region of cloud forest before emerging into bare highlands rising up to a pass. From here, the ruins of Runturacay (Egg Hut) can be seen high up at the head of the valley. The Trail drops into the valley before rising up to Runturacay, a large double-walled oval building, with a smaller rectangular structure below. The superb views indicate that this was a look-out post as well as a tambo, and the massive walls suggest that it may have had a defensive purpose.

The Trail climbs up from Runturacay and over the second pass towards Sayac-marca, which is situated on a mountain spur above, and can only be reached up a long stone stairway leading to an elevated platform at the top of the site. The main plaza is just below, with three sides of an oval tower on its west side, and the layout of the surrounding buildings is extremely dense. An aqueduct runs from the west

The Inca Bridge, about a mile from Machu Picchu, on a path leading west from the Watchman's Hut. The bridge was a defensive measure – it would have been removed when enemies threatened, leaving an impassable gap.

Above, the urban zone at Huiñay Huayna, with the series of ritual baths stepping down from the right. The name of the site means 'Forever Young', after an orchid exclusive to the area.

Below, the Uncut Rock in the quarry at Machu Picchu. It shows how Inca masons would have split a rock, using wooden wedges to widen cracks. In fact, this example was probably done by an archæologist on Bingham's expedition, testing the method.

to bring water to three ritual baths across the middle of the site, linked by an underground channel, and to a fourth outer bath, recently discovered. Sayacmarca is unusual in having no agricultural terraces; presumably its food was brought in from elsewhere. Surrounded by steep drops, it is highly defensible, and was probably a guard post, used to control traffic along the highway.

From Sayacmarca the Trail goes over the third pass, at one stage through a fissure widened into a tunnel twenty yards long, where the rock face is impassably steep. There are excellent views from the pass to the Urubamba valley; from here, the ruins of Phuyupatamarca (Town of the Clouds) are a short distance below. The Trail leads to the south-east of the site, to an enormous huaca beneath six liturgical baths fed directly from a stream. North-west of the huaca, a series of terraces follow the natural contours around the spur, connected by stone staircases. On the levelled-off top of the spur, the main plaza, a double jamb doorway has been erected, indicating that it was a very holy place. The construction of this temple was apparently abandoned, as the building is incomplete and there are no loose stones. From the south-west corner of the site, a stone stairway leads straight down the mountain towards Huiñay Huayna.

Along the way, the long staircase passes a small cave, divided by a wall with niches, and through another tunnel. The path to Huiñay Huayna leads south off the main Trail, to arrive at the north of the site, emerging from the forest at the top of a series of about ten terraces; a great many more remain hidden under the trees. The path follows round to a massive semicircular tower on the spur, from which three windows overlook the rest of the site; a small waterfall drops out of the forest over to the right. The buildings behind the tower contain a single ritual bath, and a series of ten more follows the line of the staircase below. The stairs lead down to a small urban zone at the foot of the terraces, centered on a square with two open-fronted buildings. To the east, a spectacular stone platform stands above five hundred feet or more of precipice.

From Huiñay Huayna it is a few hours walk to Intipunktu and Machu Picchu. But if time permits, the extensive terraces of Intipata above the Trail to Intipunktu make a worthwhile detour. Covering a whole hillside, Intipata was a vast centre of agricultural production.

Machu Picchu

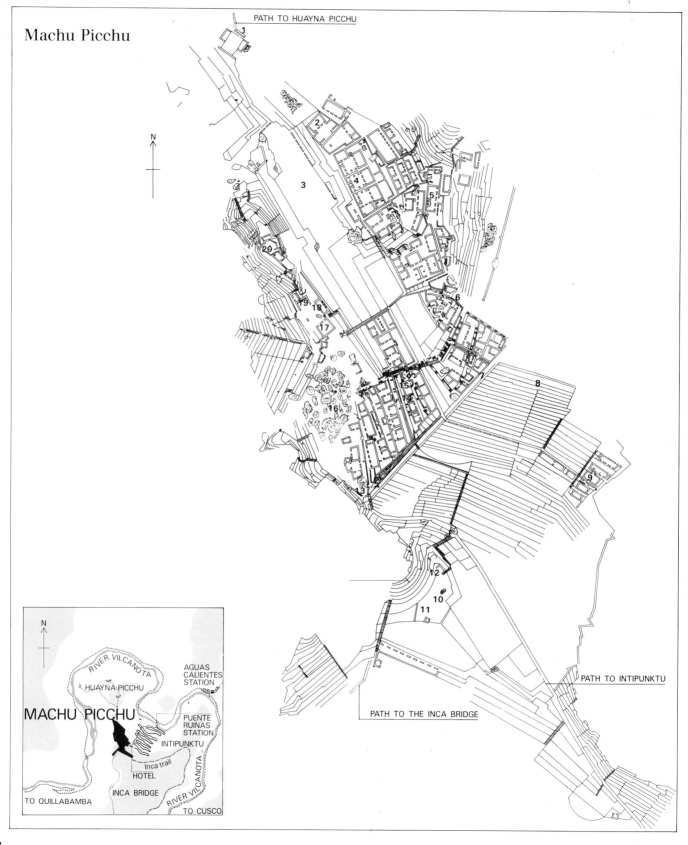

PATH TO HUAYNA PICCHU

N

1
2
3
4
5
6
7
8
9
10
11
12
13
16
17
18
19
20

PATH TO INTIPUNKTU

PATH TO THE INCA BRIDGE

N

RIVER VILCANOTA

HUAYNA PICCHU

MACHU PICCHU

AGUAS
CALIENTES
STATION

PUENTE
RUINAS
STATION

INTIPUNKTU

Inca trail

HOTEL

INCA BRIDGE

RIVER VILCANOTA

TO QUILLABAMBA

TO CUSCO

The main ruins at Machu Picchu, showing the various buildings and zones mentioned in the text. The orientation map (inset) shows the ruins in relation to the hotel and road, and the nearby sites.

key

1 *The Sacred Rock*

2 *Temple of the Moon*

3 *Main esplanade (plaza)*

4 *The Group of the Three Doorways*

5 *Industrial sector*

6 *The Condor Temple (prison)*

7 *Dry moat between agricultural sector and city*

8 *Agricultural sector*

9 *Terrace Caretaker Houses (modern entrance)*

10 *The Funerary Rock*

11 *Graveyard*

12 *The Watchman's Hut*

13 *Original Main Gate*

14 *Palace of the Princess*

15 *Temple of the Sun (The Tower) and (beneath) the Inca's Tomb*

16 *Quarry*

17 *The Sacristy*

18 *Temple of the Three Windows*

19 *Principal Temple*

20 *Intihuatana*

An area of 32,600 hectares of cloud forest around Machu Picchu has been declared a Historical Sanctuary: in spite of this, it has been greatly damaged by settlers' fires, and illegally burnt hillsides can be seen even from the train to Machu Picchu. Outside the sanctuary, the forests are under even greater threat, as huge areas are burnt off for pasture, or to make way for bananas, mangoes, maize and illegal coca plantations. Any new road is followed by an army of settlers, with neither the knowledge nor the resources to reconstruct the Inca terraces and irrigation systems on the steep mountains. The Peruvian government is either unable or unwilling to act.

It is hard to avoid the conclusion that even in our lifetimes the ongoing environmental destruction of Peru that began with the Spanish Conquest may become a catastrophe, leaving nothing but barren hillsides and starving communities. This must tinge with sadness the unforgettable experience of a visit to Machu Picchu.

City of New Castile

In March 1534, Francisco Pizarro proclaimed the founding of Cusco as a city of New Castile. Tahuantinsuyo had fallen to an aggresssive and acquisitive power, which intended both to occupy the land and exploit its people. Although weaknesses in Inca society led to its fall, the roots of the Conquest are also across the world in the kingdom of medieval Castile. Castile was formed through a long process of 're-conquest', the driving out of the Moors from the Iberian peninsula. Once this was complete, it was natural for the aristocracy and newly unemployed soldiers to turn their attention further afield. The economic and social effects of the Black Death gave added impetus. At the same time, advances in navigation and shipbuilding made it possible for adventurers and explorers to travel further than ever before.

Portuguese explorers led the way, and the Castilian conquistadors (conquerors) soon followed, establishing a presence in the Caribbean in the early sixteenth century. Some of the conquistadors were battle-hardened professional soldiers, others peasants and artesans. Although each man's primary goal was to seek individual honour and wealth, loyalty to the band of companions and its Captain was fierce. The pervasive influence of Crown and Church was always in the background; the support of both was needed to give legitimacy and moral authority to the process of conquest. Rather like the Inca, the Spanish King was seen as the representative of God on earth, and was the linchpin of the entire social order. Before a conquistador captain set out, the Crown would grant him a form of contract known as a 'capitula-cion', which apportioned the land and booty to be obtained between the two parties.

From 1519 on, the Spanish began their conquests in earnest from their Caribbean bases. There were two main thrusts: the first started with the fall of the Aztecs in 1521; the second began in Panama, then spread down the Pacific coast towards the Inca empire. By 1540 the greater part of South and Meso-America were under Spanish or Portuguese control. On the Spanish side, this was the work of no more than ten thousand men. The Crown of Castile, with perhaps six million subjects in 1519, had gained as many as 50 million more; disease and hardship would soon reduce their numbers drastically.

The mechanisms of colonization and administration were complex. The apparent overall ruler was the Viceroy, direct representative of the King. But his power was greatly circumscribed, both by the Church and by the Audiencia, a body with

The Plaza de Armas in Cusco, seen from the north-east side. The dome over the roof tops is that of the church of San Francisco.

sweeping judicial powers, including reporting to the King on the conduct of the Viceroy. Both the religious and secular administrations built up vast bureaucracies, essentially parasitical, though in their own terms effective.

In the provinces, the basic mechanism of settlement was that of 'encomienda'. All the natives in a given area would have to pay tribute to the Spanish 'encomendero'; in return, he was responsible for their conversion to Christianity. He would live a life of luxury elsewhere, leaving all the administration to a 'curaca' or native chief. In practice, the system was widely abused – in the words of one Spanish official sent to look into conditions '[the Indians] live the most wretched and miserable lives of any people on earth. As long as they are healthy they are fully occupied in working only for tribute. Even when they are sick they have no respite, and few survive their first illness, however slight. . .'

Worse still were the horrors of the silver mines at Potosí and the mercury mines at Huancavelica: a year in either was little better than a death sentence. No Indian would volunteer, so the Spanish adapted the Inca system of 'mita', conscripting a number of men from every community. As the population dropped, the mita became increasingly demanding; deaths in the mines were one of the major causes of depopulation, second only to disease and starvation. Although Viceroy de Toledo attempted to legislate in favour of native rights, he was unable to change this system – for the King of Spain, the ultimate purpose of New Castile was as a source of precious metals.

Colonial Cusco

In the first years after the Conquest, Cusco had a strategic role, both in the civil wars between the conquistadors and as a centre of operations against Inca resistance. But the capital of the export-oriented colony of New Castile needed access to the sea, and in 1535 Pizarro founded the new capital of Lima. Cusco became a provincial capital, a centre for the collection of tribute, and a stopping place on the trade route between Lima, the silver mines of Potosí, and Buenos Aires. But its great historical role had been played, and from now on was the time of Cusco's 'long sleep'. Cusco was decisively roused in 1780 by an army of peasants rebelling against Spanish rule, led by José Gabriel Tupac Amaru, a native landowner directly descended from

Contemporary painting of Cusco after the devastating earthquake of 1650. The painting now hangs in the Cathedral, and is attributed to Don Alonso Cortés de Monroy. In the foreground is the Plaza de Armas, with a crowd gathered around the crucifix of the Señor de los Temblores (Lord of the Earthquakes). This image was sent to Cusco by Charles V of Spain, and is credited with the miraculous preservation of the Cathedral in the earthquake. It is taken through the streets of Cusco every Easter Monday in commemoration of the event.

Above, the great bell of the Ascension of Our Lady in the Cathedral of Cusco. It was consecrated in 1666, but previously there had been several failed efforts at casting. Finally, a former slave, a black woman named Maria Angola, came forward and threw some fifty pounds of gold and precious stones into the crucible, thus ensuring success.

Below, detail from the church roof at Andahuaylillas, the geometric decoration showing a strong Mudéjar influence.

Opposite above, the silver Cross of the Conquest on the high altar of the church of El Triunfo. The cross was supposedly carried by the conquistador Friar Valverde at the meeting with Atahualpa immediately prior to the battle which ended in Atahualpa becoming a prisoner of the Spanish.

Opposite below left, the Baroque altar at Andahuaylillas, with the profuse ornamentation and flamboyantly decorated orders that are typical of the style.

Opposite below right, the Señor de los Temblores in its usual place in the Cathedral. It is still the subject of frenzied devotion by people from all over the Cusco region, who make long pilgrimages to beseech its miraculous intervention. Strangely, the altar and chapel of this image are sparsely ornamented in comparison to the rest of the Cathedral.

Manco Inca. Then in 1821, the Viceroy briefly made Cusco his capital, as Lima was already in the hands of armies fighting for Peruvian independence. But otherwise, Cusco was a seldom disturbed backwater.

The building of colonial Cusco only began in earnest after the end of Manco Inca's Great Rebellion. Most of the existing buildings were in ruins, and the Spanish rebuilt the city using intact Inca walls as foundations and dismantling others for their stone. Their intention was to reproduce as exactly as possible a Spanish city, although in practice colonial architecture soon took on its own rather unique character, starting with the hybrid effect of its construction on the massive Inca walls. To add to the differences, new architectural trends took perhaps half a century to filter through to the colony from Spain. More important, the indigenous craftsmen had their own traditions of stone working, and developed them in distinctive ways under their new masters. Nowhere more than Cusco are the colonial and Inca traditions melded: in places they can hardly be told apart.

Little remains of Cusco's early colonial architecture, for the great earthquake of 1650 levelled much of the city, leaving the Inca walls standing. The lessons of this were reflected in the subsequent massive, low constructions, which look flattened compared to the Spanish originals. Early colonial architecture was strongly influenced by the Mudéjar (Islamic) traditions resulting from the Arab occupation of the Iberian peninsula. This can be seen in the delicate woodwork on the balconies of Cusco's colonial houses, and the geometric decoration of flat areas in earlier churches. More rarely, it is possible to detect elements of the Gothic, with pointed arches and crenellations. But not long after the Conquest, the distant Italian High Renaissance inspired the development of the style called Plateresque, the name deriving from the Spanish word for silversmith. Without the classical purity of the original Renaissance, the style does indeed call silverwork to mind – typical features are flat surfaces decorated with medallions, restrained ornamentation, and simple classical orders.

By the time of the 1650 earthquake, the Spanish Baroque was becoming the dominant architectural style of Peru. Colonial Baroque never achieved the interplay of spatial volumes associated with the style in Europe; in the earlier years at least, it was little more than a heavily decorated variant of the Plateresque. With the energetic rebuilding that began after the earthquake, the local Baroque assumed a greater exuberance, though never going as far as the flamboyant excesses of the Churrigueresque Baroque in Spain and Mexico. The most striking example in Cusco is the tower of Santo Domingo, with its profuse helicoidal Corinthian columns and pinnacle-surrounded domes. Interestingly, the doorway beneath is more typical of the early Renaissance, and this mixing of different styles in the same building is typical of Cusco. Even in one architectural element, such as a doorway, it is quite usual to find traces of two or three colonial styles, not to mention the Inca. This is what gives Cusco its architectural richness, and makes it so hard to pin down the buildings to any particular time or style.

It was not enough to build churches; they also had to be decorated and equipped. During the seventeenth and eighteenth centuries, Cusco rose to a new prominence as a centre for the religious arts and decorative crafts. Under Spanish direction, indigenous master craftsmen perfected new skills of painting, embroidery, wood and stone carving, working precious metals and organ building.

The Plaza de Armas has always been the ceremonial and symbolic centre of Cusco. Over the centuries, it has been the stage for battles, executions, and both religious and secular celebrations. For the Spanish, its importance was such that there are three major churches and a number of chapels dominating two sides of the Plaza; the other two sides are arcaded with colonial houses.

The single battle that sealed Cusco's fate was during Manco Inca's Great Rebellion. Cusco was under siege, and the Spanish defenders were sheltering in Sunturhuasi, the Inca armoury which stood on what is now the southern corner of the Plaza. Red-hot stones rained down on Cusco's thatched roofs, burning most of the city, but Sunturhuasi somehow escaped and eventually the rebels were defeated. The event soon acquired miraculous status, and the Virgin Mary and her archangels were said to have extinguished the flames. There is another explanation – the negro slaves stationed on the roof with buckets of water. To commemorate the Spanish victory, a temporary cathedral was built on the site of Sunturhuasi. In 1730, the existing church of El Triunfo (The Triumph) replaced it. The church contains eighteenth-century paintings depicting the celestial fire brigade in action.

The Cathedral stands next to El Triunfo, on the site of the main part of Viracocha's

Left, anonymous eighteenth-century painting of the Virgin and Child in the Cusco Museum of Religious Art. It shows the distinctive technique of 'brocateado', the superimposition of a lacework of gold lines and shapes over paintwork, that was widely used in the Cusco School of painting.

Right, portrait of Bishop Mollinedo, by one of the leading painters of the Cusco School, Diego Quispe Tito, in the Cusco Museum of Religious Art.

palace. Planning began in 1559, but its construction was delayed by the building of deep foundations into the marshy ground. It was still incomplete in 1650, when the earthquake caused minor damage, and not consecrated until 1669. The Cathedral has an intricate Baroque doorway, flanked by two massive and squat towers. The interior is cool and dark, with a wide stone vaulted roof over the main nave. The Plateresque choir-stalls are a good example of early wood carving. Otherwise, the main interest is in the nearly four hundred colonial paintings that decorate the walls of the Cathedral, and in the Baroque altars and other works of art in the side chapels. The small chapel to the left of the Cathedral is that of Jesus, Mary and Joseph, built in 1733. Many of the paintings in the Cathedral are of the Cusco School, which flourished throughout the sixteenth and seventeenth centuries. Its work was famous all over the continent, and reached as far as Quito, Buenos Aires and Santiago, though most remained in Peru. Some of the studios became little more than production lines, turning out three or four large canvases a day. One important artist was the Italian Jesuit Bernado Bitti, who had been trained in Rome and passed on his techniques to native painters and craftsmen.

Another leading artistic figure was Bishop Mollinedo, who came from Spain in 1673, bringing paintings with him. When these were copied by indigenous painters, they would often add their own touches; for example, in the painting of the Last Supper in the nave of the Cathedral, Jesus and his apostles are sitting down to a meal of 'cuy' (guinea pig) as they might have done at an Inca banquet. Mollinedo had a number of new churches built, and commissioned artistic works for existing churches, showing an impressive ability to raise the enormous sums required from the wealthy of Cusco. He was largely responsible for the artistic flowering of the late seventeenth century, the most creative and productive period in Cusco's colonial history.

The important church on the south-west side of the Plaza is that of La Compañía, named after its builders, the Jesuits, the 'Compañía de Jesus'. When the original sixteenth-century church and monastery on the site were seriously damaged in the 1650 earthquake, the Jesuits deliberately chose to rebuild a church of a splendour to rival the Cathedral. With its great dome, Baroque high altar, and the graceful ensemble of the towers and main doorway, it would be hard to judge between the two. The Pope himself intervened, ordering the Jesuits to halt construction, but by then the church was complete. The monastery was declared a University by the Pope in 1622. With a façade almost as richly embellished as that of its neighbour, the now University of Cusco retains a cloistered courtyard built of brick and adobe on stone bases, an example of early colonial construction.

The northern quarter of Cusco, built on the slopes below Sacsayhuaman, keeps its traditional character more than any other: its narrow and often stepped streets tend to exclude motor vehicles. Leaving the Plaza along Calle del Almirante, left of the Cathedral, the Casa del Almirante is prominent on the corner above. This is the house, or palace, where Admiral Maldonado lived from 1629, as both Mayor and Governor of Cusco. The house was rebuilt around its large cloistered courtyard after serious damage in the 1650 earthquake. From 1821–3 it was the residence of the last Viceroy before his final defeat by the forces of independence. It has been restored since the 1950 earthquake to become the Museum of Regional History and now houses a substantial collection of religious paintings of the Cusco School. The interior is known especially for its grand staircase with statues of mythical beasts, and for the painted and coffered ceilings.

A few minutes walk up Calle Tucuman beyond the Casa del Almirante is the small, plain-fronted Plazoleta de las Nazarenas, which existed in Inca times under the name of Amarukjata (Slope of the Snakes). For its size, the Plazoleta has a good number of colonial buildings. On the corner with Tucuman is the Casa de la Torre, built in stages over the sixteenth and seventeenth centuries. Behind the plain façade with its ornamented Plateresque doorway, a central courtyard has two levels of Mudéjar arches. The unrestored house contrasts strongly with the next building around the square, the Casa de Cabrera. Built around two large courtyards one behind the other, this house has recently been restored by a bank, and now houses a private art gallery and archaeological museum with many Inca artefacts.

The large building at the north of the plazoleta is the convent of Las Nazarenas, also known as the Casa de las Sierpes (House of Serpents). Its walls are carved with serpents, an Inca symbol of learning and intelligence, commemorating the site's original purpose as a school for the education of the sons of Inca nobles. After the Conquest the site was allotted to conquistador Mancio de Leguizamo, who boasted

Canchipata, a typical narrow stepped street in the northern quarter of Cusco.

The Plateresque doorway of the Casa del Almirante, unusually positioned on a corner, ornamented with rosettes and a coat of arms and flanked by Inca-influenced masonry. The small balcony above looks out over the Plaza de Armas and the central column is carved in the form of a hermaphrodite, with Janus faces looking both ways. Admiral Maldonado is reputed to have sent Indians to their deaths if they looked up at him standing on the balcony. He was found one day mysteriously hanging by the neck inside the house.

Above, the courtyard of the interesting but unrestored Casa La Torre at Plaza Nazarenas 211, in multiple occupation by a number of families.

Right, the elegant two-storey cloister of the monastery of San Francisco, built almost entirely with stones from Inca palaces that stood on the site.

Above, the cloister of the monastery of La Merced, an oasis of tranquility in Cusco's bustling commercial district.

Below, relief carvings of pumas on the façade of the colonial Casa de las Pumas, one of several houses in varying states of repair along the Calle Santa Teresa from the Plaza Regocijo.

Courtyard of a colonial house at Calle Marquez 215, unrestored but in reasonable condition.

of discovering the great Punchao from Coricancha – and losing it at dice the same night. The house was converted to a lodge for the Order of the Barefoot Nazarenes in 1747, and in 1760 it became a monastery, with the addition of a chapel and other buildings. Despite its spacious interior built around seven patios, it is most notable for its simple but elegant belltower and its doorway built by native stonemasons soon after the Conquest.

Across the narrow alleyway of Siete Culebras (Seven Snakes) is the old seminary of San Antonio Abad. It is known for its porch onto the plazoleta, with the coat of arms of Bishop Mollinedo under an unusual oval window. Siete Culebras leads under a high arch between the two buildings, running between their walls of well-preserved Inca masonary before reaching the Calle Choquechaca, which contains many colonial houses with interesting façades and entrances. The road is stepped as it climbs steeply towards a rock outcrop, and has a good view of Cusco. Judging from the remnants of Inca stonework, this was also a ceremonial site. However, the pretty arched stone aqueduct that crosses the Tullumayu is definitely colonial.

The church of San Cristóbal and the ruins of the palace of Colcampata are a short distance to the south-west, at a similar altitude. After the defeat of Manco Inca's rebellion, Colcampata was taken over by his brother Paullu Inca, so active a collaborator with Spanish rule that the Spanish themselves were bemused – he even joined Gonzalo Pizarro's expedition to crush Manco's kingdom of Vilcabamba. He readily converted to Christianity, and built a chapel on the site of the larger present church.

After Paullu's death, Colcampata passed to his son Carlos Inca, but in his determination to destroy the cult of the Incas, Viceroy de Toledo expropriated Carlos, and turned Colcampata into a prison and fortress. In this role Colcampata briefly housed Carlos' cousin, Tupac Amaru, defeated at Vilcabamba and imprisoned here until his execution. The King later restored Carlos's estates, which eventually passed to his son Melchor, a pathetic figure who died of melancholy in Spain. From Colcampata it is only a short walk up to Sacsayhuaman. On the way down, the region of narrow streets between Colcampata and the Plaza de Armas is full of Inca stonework and run-down colonial houses.

The western part of Cusco had few buildings at the time of the Conquest, which

Detail of the brightly coloured mural paintings in the Capitular Room at the convent of Santa Catalina. The theme of the murals is the contrast between the holy life of the saints and more worldly pleasures. Here we see Saint Gerónimo surrounded by adoring wildlife as he conducts a self-imposed penitence. Beneath, a group of hunters are enjoying a spot of mayhem with God's creatures.

Above, The Baptism of Jesus, one of many fine colonial paintings on religious themes in the convent of Santa Catalina. The artist was Diego Quispe Tito, or one of his followers.

Below, Statue of the Virgin being carried in the procession for Corpus Christi. Early eighteenth-century painting by Diego Quispe Tito, now in the Cusco Museum of Religious Art.

gave the Spanish the opportunity to build on a wide street plan, suitable for horses and wheeled traffic, and also, unfortunately, for the motor car.

The small but charming Plaza Regocijo, just west of the Plaza de Armas, is nearly all that remains of Cusipata, the Inca Square of Joy. Little is known of the Inca buildings around Cusipata; many sources even show the surrounding area as fields, but this is clearly inaccurate as traces of Inca masonry remain to this day. The most prominent example is the imposing Cabildo, on the north-west side of Plaza Regocijo, which stands on lower walls of Inca stonework, stretching for the entire block, and is entered through a large Inca portal. The magnificent workmanship indicates that the Inca building on the site was important. The Inca walls are now under a colonial arcade, and the central patio is graced by fountains. The Cabildo was the centre of local government throughout the colonial period, was restored in the nineteenth century and is now Cusco's Prefecture.

Nearby, on Calle Garcilaso, at the south corner of the Plaza Regocijo, is the Casa Garcilaso, named after the swashbuckling conquistador Garcilaso de la Vega. In fact, the house on the site today dates from the late seventeenth century, although Garcilaso may have lived here in an earlier house with his wife, the Inca Princess Isabel. Their son, the chronicler Garcilaso de la Vega Inca, was born in 1539. He learnt a great deal of Inca history and traditions from his mother and carefully observed the changes taking place as he grew to adulthood. After his father's death, when Garcilaso was twenty, he travelled to Spain and remained there until his death. It was only as an old man that he began to write his great work, *The Royal Commentaries of the Incas*, for many years the principal historical source about the Incas and the Conquest.

Casa Garcilaso has now been thoroughly restored as an office of the Instituto Nacional de Cultura (INC). Just opposite Casa Garcilaso is the Casa Jara, one of the best preserved of Cusco's colonial houses. Built during the seventeenth and eighteenth centuries by the descendants of conquistador Jara de la Cerda, it is now a guest house. A look through the porch, built of Inca stones beneath the seventeenth-century wooden balcony, reveals an attractive patio with arches of stone and brick.

Calle Garcilaso leads through to the exclusively colonial Plaza San Francisco, an area which was under agricultural terraces at the time of the Conquest. The square

The finest example of Cusco's Baroque wood carving is the profusely decorated pulpit in the church of San Blas, two blocks north west of the Archbishop's Palace. The church itself is of no great interest, but the pulpit, commissioned by Bishop Mollinedo, is a masterpiece. In this detail the Virgin Mary is flanked by intricate, almost rococo carvings. Just out of sight beneath her is a series of scowling heretics and blasphemers, painfully bearing the weighty edifice above.

takes its name from the large Franciscan church and monastery on the western corner, founded in 1534. After the 1650 earthquake, many of the still incomplete buildings had to be rebuilt. Little remains now of the once elaborate interior, which was stripped out by the friars at the beginning of this century. Only the cedar-wood choir and pulpit survived, superbly carved by indigenous craftsmen in the mid-seventeenth century.

North-west from Plaza Regocijo up Calle Santa Teresa are the church and convent of Santa Teresa, built on Inca foundations of unknown origin. The convent was founded in 1661, while the church was not finished until 1678. Bishop Mollinedo played an important part in the decoration of the church, commissioning the silver altar piece, tabernacle, monstrance and crucifix, and some of the paintings; he was eventually laid to rest in the crypt.

West of the church across the small Plaza de Silvaq is the Casa Silva, Viceroy de Toledo's temporary home following his arrival in Cusco in 1571. Here Tupac Amaru was brought captive and bound in gold chains, and led under the window where de Toledo was standing. Tupac Amaru refused to bow his head, and was beaten for his insolence. The portal, with its monolithic jambs and Baroque helicoidal columns, is flanked by Inca stonework of unknown origin.

The most important buildings in the commercial district to the south of the Plaza are those of the church and monastery of La Merced, only a short distance down Calle Marquez. The foundations date from 1536, just two years after Cusco's Spanish foundation. The present buildings mostly date from the late seventeenth century, as the earlier ones were levelled in the 1650 earthquake. La Merced was constructed on a grand scale, especially the enormous staircase between the two cloisters with its huge tree of life painting of the Mercedarian Order: the building served as headquarters for the Order throughout South America until 1700.

The two entrance lobbies contain interesting paintings, including one of a rather unfair intervention by Santiago (St James) in a battle between conquistadors and Indians. De Almagro and his son, together with Gonzalo Pizarro, lie buried in crypts under the church – a small collection of Spanish rebels. Above, the nave reaches a height of over fifty feet, its walls hung with numerous paintings, some a little grotesque to modern eyes. The well-watered garden at the centre of the two-storey

Two typical examples of the unassuming and simple colonial architecture in the villages of the Cusco region: the main square of Checacupe and the main square at Quiquijana, both in the upper valley of the Vilcanota.

*The doorways respectively to the bell tower and Sacristy at
Andahuaylillas, in contrasting states of repair — money for
restoration ran out when only a small part of the work had been done.*

AY DEMI QUE ARDIENDO QUEDO AY QUE PUDE YANOPUEDO

Detail from 'Heaven and Hell' at Huaro. Among the inhabitants of the cauldron are a bishop, a cardinal, and a friar – a subversive message for a society in which the Church had almost unfettered powers.

cloister, surrounded by Corinthian columns of pink granitic stone, is a tranquil place. A sequence of paintings around the lower cloister shows scenes in the life of the Order's founder, San Pedro de Nolasco. Just off the cloisters, a small museum contains a large gold monstrance of 1806 and some important paintings, among them a Rubens.

Just beyond La Merced is the mansion of the Marques de Valleumbroso, badly damaged both in the 1950 earthquake and in a 1973 fire, and still awaiting full restoration. Its ornamental portal is an interesting hybrid of styles: the massive doorway with inclined jambs was evidently built by Inca stonemasons, probably after the Conquest. It is flanked by treble pilasters, repeated above with a balcony between, topped by the Valleumbroso coat of arms.

The eastern part of Cusco was, in Inca times, the real centre of the city. Remains of some of the public buildings in this area are visible to this day. For example, Calle Loreto, the narrow alley between the Plaza and Coricancha, still gives an excellent impression of how Cusco's streets must have looked before the Conquest. High walls of cut and fitted stone rise on both sides: Huayna Capac's palace on the right, now La Compañía; the House of the Sun Virgins, now the convent of Santa Catalina, on the left.

The convent and church of Santa Catalina were finished soon after the 1650 earthquake. Although still a convent, the complex houses a large museum, entered from Calle Santa Catalina, parallel with Calle Loreto. The museum contains an excellent collection of religious art by anonymous Indian artists of Cusco. A low-ceilinged chamber on the ground floor is decorated with bright murals contrasting the life of worldly pleasures with the holy life of the saints. On the grand staircase a huge carpet depicts a Tree of Life with two Spaniards cutting it down – an intriguing metaphor.

Turning left onto Calle Santa Catalina Ancha, the impressive building on the right is the Casa Concha, which stands on the lower walls of Pucamarca, the palace of Tupac Yupanqui. The house belonged to many generations of Canchas, including the last Governor of Cusco before independence. It has since become the local Police Headquarters and casual visitors are not encouraged.

There are more Inca walls along Pampa de Castillo, the continuation of Calle

Loreto, with Inca-influenced colonial doorways leading through to the houses behind. Pampa de Castillo leads out into the open space in front of the church and monastery of Santo Domingo, built over the ruins of Coricancha. The church dates from 1681, though some pre-1650 fragments remain. Severe damage sustained in the 1950 earthquake revealed many Inca walls and foundations, and it is usually these and other remains of Coricancha that most impress visitors to Santo Domingo, although the church is of considerable interest in its own right.

Just north of Santo Domingo on Calle San Agustín is the Casa de los Cuatro Bustos, now a hotel, but it is possible to look around. A few blocks north-west, behind the church of El Triunfo, is the Archbishop's Palace, once the house of the conquistador-bishop Valverde. The original building, Inca Roca's palace, was pulled to pieces by gold hunters and then used as a quarry, and only its great outer walls remain. A look around this building, which the archbishop now shares with the Museum of Religious Art, gives an idea of the luxury enjoyed by high-ranking colonial clerics.

A final example of Cusco's Baroque wood carving, also the greatest, is the profusely decorated pulpit in the church of San Blas, two blocks north west from the Archbishop's Palace. The church itself is not of great interest, but the pulpit, commissioned by Bishop Mollinedo, is a masterpiece. Most interesting to modern observers are the six scowling heretics and blasphemers at its base, painfully bearing the weighty edifice above.

Huaro and Andahuaylillas

The villages and towns around Cusco all have their colonial houses, bridges and churches, many in advanced disrepair. There are two churches that stand out above the rest, sited south of Cusco near Pikillacta in the villages of Andahuaylillas and Huaro. The churches are unremarkable, but the murals inside offer an unforgettable vision of death, torment and hell – a unique insight into the religious mentality of the late eighteenth century, and of the impact of Christianity on the native population. The painter in both was probably Tadeo Escalante, an indigenous artist trained in Cusco.

The interior of the church at Andahuaylillas, with its huge silver-covered Baroque altar, the carved pulpit, the Mudéjar roof, and the series of eight large canvases on

Above, detail from the series of murals at Huaro with Death as the central theme. In this case, Death is reaching out from beneath a bed to seize the vestments of a passing priest.

Left, doorway to the bell tower at Huaro – above, devils are breaking sinners on the wheel. Originally, the murals extended down to the floor, but were whitewashed over in the nineteenth century so as to avoid distracting the congregation.

the walls of the nave show that the village was more prosperous than now. The organ is decorated with faded paintings of angels, and most of the remaining wall space is covered in mural decoration. At the back of the church is Escalante's 'Heaven and Hell'. As always, Hell looks more interesting, with a huge monster devouring the wicked and devils and skeletons prancing around.

The murals at Huaro are more numerous with an obsessional and disturbing quality and a freshness that sets them apart. Huaro was traditionally a centre of witchcraft, so maybe the intention of the murals was to terrify the locals into virtuous ways. The vision of Hell, on the right of the church at the back, was certainly based on the torture chambers of the Spanish Inquisition. One fascinating detail is that the three executioners of the 1780 rebel leader Gabriel Tupac Amaru are themselves undergoing appalling torments. We can only assume that Escalante himself sympathized with the uprising. In the murals opposite, death is an ever-present theme – in the house of a poor man, at the banquet of a rich man, with young lovers, and at the Resurrection and final judgement. The murals are in a poor state of repair, damp, and on crumbling plaster. Some restoration has been carried out, but there is no money to finish the work.

It is nearly a thousand years since Manco Inca chose Cusco as home for the Incas. Over the centuries, Cusco has been built, destroyed, and rebuilt many times. As its second millenium approaches, both construction and destruction are under way at a feverish pace. Just as the Spanish destroyed Inca Cusco, so the twentieth century is threatening to destroy colonial Cusco. The 1950 earthquake damaged many colonial buildings; many were then bulldozed, not because they were beyond repair, but to take advantage of reconstruction credits. Modern buildings of concrete have taken their place. On Cusco's outskirts, huge areas are under construction, unplanned settlements of mud-brick and corrugated iron. The now defunct 1951 reconstruction plan, with its bold orbital road and radial avenues to the Plaza de Armas, would have done more damage still. The plan also included new towns at Machu Picchu, Pisac, and Ollantaytambo.

The theme of destruction has been a constant one in this book. Visitors to Cusco and the surrounding Inca sites cannot avoid becoming aware of the continuing

The church at Huaro, looking back towards the organ gallery. The mural shows Christ being taken off the Cross, one of the less disturbing images in the church. The blue confessional boxes date from the later colonial period, while the canvases over are in such poor condition that it is almost impossible to make out their subjects.

erosion of the environment and cultural heritage, through ignorance, poverty and greed. It is harder to find those Peruvians and others who are struggling to reverse the trend, but they are there. One thing is certain, that without tourism the chances for preservation and restoration would be slim indeed. Tourism is always a double-edged sword: though it highlights social tensions and inequalities, it also brings resources and keeps problems in view.

Travellers' Information

When to go

The rainy season, from November to April, brings torrential rain and muddy roads, but fewer people, lower prices, more hotel vacancies and green hills. The best (though crowded) time is in May or June, with sun, clear skies, and still green vegetation. It is a good idea to time a visit to coincide with one of the fiestas – see below.

Travel Documents

For citizens of most countries, including Britain and the USA, a visa is granted on arrival valid for 30, 60 or 90 days. Extending the visa can be very tedious.

Insurance

Travel insurance is indispensable, as there are many pickpockets and other thieves (mostly non-violent). Flight delay cover is a good idea, as internal flights are subject to frequent cancellation.

Costs

Peru is cheap, but it is difficult to give accurate prices due to rampant inflation. US dollars should be taken in a mix of cash (small bills) and traveller's cheques. Credit cards are useful for air tickets, hotel bills (check first) and in some shops. A budget traveller can survive on $100 a month, but it is possible to spend as much in a day.

Health Precautions

Typhoid and hepatitis (gamma globulin) vaccinations and polio and tetanus boosters are advised. For lowland jungle areas (not Machu Picchu) add yellow fever and take a supply of malaria prophylactics. It is a good idea to take a full first aid kit, with adequate supplies of any regularly needed medicines. Sun lotion and diarrhoea pills are certain to be needed. High altitudes make Cusco and the surrounding area unsuitable for those suffering from any form of heart and lung condition. Health insurance with full repatriation cover is very important.

Clothes and Equipment

The weather in Cusco is variable. Nights are cold, with frosts during June, July and August, and days are often hot, with strong sunshine. During the rainy season, heavy rain is often interspersed with sunshine. Rain can fall at any time of year. A good range of clothing, including waterproofs, is needed. Specialist equipment is needed for trekkers on the Inca and other Trails. Weather conditions are more extreme at high altitude; a good sleeping bag and waterproof tent, boots and clothing are essential – and a pair of shorts. Equipment can be hired in Cusco but the standard is often inadequate.

Organized Tours

A number of UK based companies offer comprehensive tours to Peru. Latin American Experience (Tel: 01–379 0344), Journey Latin America (01–747 3108), Trailfinders (01–603 1515) and Encounter Overland (01–370 6845) all offer both simple tickets and a range of tour options. Serenissima and Heritage Travel Ltd. (01–730 9841) offer a comprehensive tour of Peru and Bolivia.

By air

There are no long distance flights to Cusco – Lima is the usual staging point. All internal flights to the highlands leave early in the morning to avoid turbulence. Flights from Lima and Arequipa (Aeroperu, Faucett) daily, flights from Juliaca (Faucett, Aeroperu) weekly, flights from La Paz (Lloyd Aereo Bolivia) twice weekly. Cash dollars is the preferred method of payment. Foreigners pay a different rate from Peruvian residents, at least double. Credit cards can work out as a bargain, due to devaluation, but some agencies will attempt to add a surcharge. Travellers' cheques are more of a problem; the only places to accept them at face value are Faucett offices. Long delays, cancellations, and technical problems are frequent on all lines, but flying is still preferable to the bus. At busy times, it is best to confirm and reconfirm travel, and to be at the airport early.

By Bus

From Cusco, bus services run to Puno, Juliaca, Arequipa, and on to Lima, La Paz, etc, and are very cheap. The journeys are long, uncomfortable and subject to frequent delays, particularly in the rainy season. Routes passing through the strife torn departments of Ayacucho and Apurímac are dangerous, too.

By Train

A daily train service runs to and from Puno, Arequipa and Juliaca, leaving early in the morning and arriving in the evening or night. Tickets are available in Tourist, First and Second Class, and may be bought through an agent or from the station on the day before – check times. First and Second Class are very cheap, but full of thieves. Tourist Class is more expensive, but has an armed guard in each carriage. These trains arrive at the Huanchác station in Cusco's south-east suburbs.

By Car

See 'By Bus'. Car hire is possible, but not recommended. Hazards include army and police checkpoints, infrequent petrol stations and breakdowns. Four-wheel drive necessary, especially in the rainy season.

The means of travel around Cusco are train, bus, truck, taxi and tourist minibus. All public transport is very cheap, and cheapest of the lot are trucks, the only way of reaching some destinations. The cost of taxis to places outside Cusco is highly variable, in the range US$20–50 per day, and worth negotiating before departure. Within Cusco there are low standard rates. Buses leave from Cusco to many destinations, and the bus stations are spread around the edges of the city – enquire at the tourist office.

Machu Picchu

The only way to reach Machu Picchu (other than walking) is by train; regulations now require that tourists buy a combined train and entry ticket to Machu Picchu, costing about US$70; some may avoid this by travelling on the train from Ollantaytambo. Trains for Ollantaytambo and Machu Picchu leave from Santa Ana station south west from the Plaza de Armas along Calle Marquez/Santa Clara.

South from Cusco

There are currently no organized tours south of Cusco; taxi or bus are recommended as trains are slow, infrequent and unreliable. Buses leave from outside the Huanchac station throughout the day.

Organized Tours

There are organized tours of Cusco, Sacsayhuaman, Quenqo, Tambo Machay and Puca Pucara, and of the Sacred Valley from Pisac to Ollantaytambo, incorporating Chinchero. Other such tours south of Cusco and into the Lares Valley are under preparation. Information about these tours is available from the Tourist Office, which regulates the prices. Such tours are recommended only as an introduction or for visitors on a tight schedule. There are a great many possible treks into the mountains near Cusco, in addition to the well-walked Inca Trail to Machu Picchu. A number of companies can arrange trips with guides, porters and all necessary food and equipment. One experienced and reliable company is Tambo Treks (Tel: 237718).

The Rainforest

A trip into the Amazon rainforest is easily arranged from Cusco. Facilities are most developed near Puerto Maldonado, a half hour's flight away at the foot of the Andes. For an authentic rainforest experience, the Explorers' Inn in the 5,500 hectare Tambopata Reserved Zone is recommended. Reservations and enquiries at most agencies or the Peruvian Safaris office on Plaza San Francisco (Tel: Cusco 313047, Telex 20416 PESAFARI Lima).

Rafting

Most Cusco travel agencies can arrange exhilarating river rafting on the Vilcanota, ending at Pisac with time to look at the ruins.

Riding

There are plenty of horses in the countryside around Cusco, and it is possible to hire them by the day either through an agency or directly from their owners. Trips especially worth making on horseback are from Ollantaytambo to Pumamarca and beyond, and from Sacsayhuaman up the grassy valleys to Tambo Machay. Rates are from around $5 per day.

Hotels

Cusco has a great range of hotels in all price brackets; only the most expensive ones can be reserved from abroad – a good idea from June to August. El Libertador (Tel. 231961, Calle San Agustín), Colonial Palace (232151, Calle Qera), Marqueses (232512, Calle Garcilaso) and the Royal Inca (222284, Plaza Regocijo) are all up-market hotels in interesting colonial houses, with prices in the region US$10–70 per night. Cheaper hotels are available from $0.50.

Outside Cusco accommodation is easy to find, but basic. An exception is El Albergue, by the station in Ollantaytambo (reservations 223350), a very pleasant place to stay. For visitors to Machu Picchu, there are basic hotels at Aguas Calientes, and a government run hotel at the ruins, bookable through travel agencies in Cusco or Lima.

Restaurants & Nightlife

There are plenty of restaurants in Cusco, offering everything from pizza to chifa (Chinese/Peruvian food), and 'international' dishes. Eating out is cheap, nowhere more so than in the local eating houses known as picanterías, of which there is a good selection up Calle Macurco. As a general rule, if somewhere looks clean and has a few Peruvians eating there, it should be worth a try. Uncooked vegetables should be avoided. One establishment worth a special mention is the Cafe Ayllu on the Plaza de Armas, serving drinks and snacks only.

A number of discos and bars operate into the small hours, some with live Andean music, audible from the street. The Crossed Keys 'pub', upstairs near the east corner of the Plaza de Armas, is a convivial spot; also the Bilboquet, Calle Herrajes, which doubles as a Creperie.

Information

Information is available at the Tourist Office on the east corner of the Plaza de Armas, situated under the Tourist Police Office (Portal de Belén 113), and books and maps can be obtained from various bookshops – 'Los Andes', on the north-west face of the Plaza de Armas (Portal Commercio 125) has a good selection. The Institute of Inca Research (Tel: 221703) can advise on trips to more remote sites, and have good maps of most; they charge a fee for this service.

Money

At time of writing, the currency is the Inti (I/), equal to 1,000 Soles, the previous unit. The exchange rate, and prices, change every day. Changing money on the street or in 'Casas de Cambio' (exchange offices) is legal and generally safe: better rates are given for cash, but lower rates for cheques, than in a bank. They are also a lot faster – it can take over an hour in Cusco's Banco de Crédito (Av Sol 189), at time of writing the only bank to change traveller's cheques. Outside Cusco, traveller's cheques and high denomination notes (dollars or Intis) are hard to change.

Health

Many people get diarrhoea at some stage – it is best to stop eating and drink plenty; and most are affected by the altitude (11,500 ft) in their first few days in Cusco, and feel weak and quickly get out of breath. Coca leaf tea – mate de coca can help. Some chemists have remedies for more serious symptons of soroche (altitude sickness) and other drugs; doctor's prescriptions are not necessary, although caution is. In case of severe illness, repatriation is advisable, as local medical facilities are best avoided. Hotels keep lists of doctors and clinics.

Timezones

Time in Peru is five hours behind Greenwich Mean Time.

Laws and Regulations

Tourists are not usually bothered by the police, but passport or a notarized photocopy should be carried at all times. Drugs such as marijuana and cocaine are on offer, but best avoided as offenders are likely to spend a long time in gaols that make Alcatraz look like a luxury hotel. Smuggling archaeological remains out of Peru is also forbidden.

Access to Museums and Sites

Most museums and sites in and around Cusco and the Sacred Valley are entered on the same ticket, costing $10 and valid for 5 days. The Inca Trail ticket is also $10, payable at the start of the hike, and does not include Machu Picchu, for which the one day ticket is another $10. Hours vary, but most sites and museums are open from 9.30 a.m. to 6.00 p.m., and museums often close from 12.30 p.m. to 2.30 p.m. Many of the less visited sites, like those south of Cusco, are unsupervised.

Shopping

Cusco is a great place for buying hand made goods, especially chompas (jumpers), ponchos, and mantas (small blankets), the best of which are made of alpaca wool. There is also some good silver jewellery at low prices. The biggest problem is getting things home without exceeding baggage allowances. Places to shop include the shops near the plaza (expensive); the many vendors under the arcades of the Plaza de Armas and Plaza Regocijo (less expensive); the craft market in the main Cusco market near the Santa Ana railway station (cheaper); and the Sunday markets in Chinchero and Pisac (similar prices to Cusco). The best bargains are available at fiesta time, when the Plaza de Armas is covered with stalls. Bargaining is the rule everywhere.

Laundry

There are no launderettes in Cusco, but a number of establishments near the Plaza which offer a six-hour service. Payment is by weight.

Photography

An ultra-violet filter is essential to accommodate the bright light. Film is available in Peru, but is often of poor quality, or past the 'sell by' date. As many Peruvians resent being photographed, they should be asked first, and then paid a propina (tip).

Robbery

The price of a good holiday in Cusco is eternal vigilance. All valuables should be concealed in inaccessible pockets or pouches. Money-belts are well known to thieves, and should not be used for passports, air tickets, etc.

Electric Current

Electricity is supplied at nominal 220 Volts, 60 Cycles; plugs are 2 pin, round or flat.

Telephone & Telex

It is possible to phone anywhere in the world from Cusco, either by private phone or from the ENTEL telephone office at 382 Avenida Sol. Calls may either be timed (3 minute minimum) or can be paid for with tokens – fichas – bought at the office. Local calls are very cheap, but international and long distance calls can be expensive. Telex facilities are also available at ENTEL, or by arrangement with hotels and offices, many of which have their own facilities.

Post

The Cusco post office is way down Avenida Sol, on the corner with Avenida Garcilaso. It often runs out of stamps, and mail then has to be franked at the office. Poste Restante is unreliable. It is possible to send parcels up to 2kg from here, sewn up in cloth and with clearance from the aduana (customs) at 344 Calle Teatro. Larger parcels can be sent through customs only. Things do seem to arrive.

Fiestas

This is only a short list of the main festivals – every village has its own Saint's Day, always an occasion for celebration.

New Year's Day	1 January	Cusco
Festival of the Magi	6 January	Ollantaytambo
Festival of San Hilarion	14 January	Pampamarca
Festival of San Sebastián	20 January	San Sebastian
Holy Week	Week up to Easter	Everywhere
Señor de los Temblores Procession	Easter Monday	Cusco
Corpus Christi	Mid-June	Cusco
Viracocha Music Festival	16–22 June	Raqchi
Señor de Qoylloriti Pilgrimage	18–19 June	Upper Vilcanota
Inti Raymi	24 June	Sacsayhuaman
Virgin of Carmen	16 July	Paucartambo
Festival of San Lorenzo	10 August	Checacupe
Festival of San Bartolomé	14 August	Tiobamba
Village Festival	15 August	Calca
Huarachicoy	Last Sunday in Aug	Sacsayhuaman
Huanca Pilgrimage	14 September	Huanca
All Saints' Day	1 November	Cusco
Festival of the Rosary	4 November	Combapata
Christmas Eve	24 December	Cusco
Christmas Day	25 December	Yucay

Useful Addresses

Cusco

American Express, c/o Lima Tours, 561 Avenida Sol.
Faucett Peruvian Airlines, 567 Avenida Sol. Tel. 233541.
Aeroperu, Avenida Sol/Calle Matara. Tel. 233051.
Lloyd Aereo Boliviano, 348 Avenida Sol. Tel. 222990.
VISA Agent, Banco de Crédito, 189 Avenida Sol.
MasterCard agent, c/o Hirca Tours, 230 Calle Garcilaso de la Vega. Tel. 227051.
Tourist office and Police, 113 Portal de Belén (west corner of Plaza de Armas). Tel. 221961.

British Embassy, Edificio Pacífico, Plaza Washington, Lima 100. Tel. Lima 334738.

Chronology

Prehistory

30,000 BC   *First archaeological evidence (disputed) of human beings in the Americas.*

15,000 BC   *First evidence of man in Peru, in caves near Ayacucho.*

12,000 BC   *Date of stone hunting weapons found near Lima.*

10,000 BC   *Glaciers retreat from the high valleys of the Andes.*

Incipient Era

8,000 BC   *Evidence of cave-dwelling hunters in Andes – cave paintings and advanced stone tools.*

5,000 BC   *First agriculture along coast and in mountains; permanent settlements along coast.*

Early Formative Era

4,000 BC   *Cultivation of maize; evidence of ceramics and weaving. Larger villages and ceremonial centres emerge; organized social structure and religion.*

1,200 BC   *Growth of the Chavín cult in northern Andes and of 'Paracas' culture on southern coast; large ceremonial centres at Chavín de Huantar and other locations. Stonework and metalwork evolve.*

Late Formative Era

300 BC   *Decline of Chavín; regional diversification of other cultures. Irrigated agriculture begins. Highly sophisticated weaving and ceramics, especially in Paracas area. First development of Tiwanaku and other cultures around lake Titicaca.*

Classical Era

AD 100   *Distinct cultures develop in different areas of Peru. Era of high artistic attainment, especially ceramics in the Moche and Nazca cultures. Golden age of Tiwanaku. Decline towards end of era.*

AD 800   *Wari Empire based near Ayacucho emerges; strong connections to now decadent Tiwanaku.*

1000   *Tiwanaku and Wari empires finally disintegrate, giving rise to diverse regional kingdoms.*

Inca Empire

1000/1200   *First Inca Manco Capac founds Cusco and the Inca kingdom.*

1438   *Ninth Inca Pachacutec initiates major conquests. Comprehensive reconstruction of Cusco and Sacsayhuaman.*

1471   *Tenth Inca Tupac Yupanqui continues imperial expansion to conquer most of modern Peru, Ecuador, Bolivia, half of Chile and parts of Argentina and Colombia.*

1492   *Christopher Columbus arrives in the Americas.*

1493   *Huayna Capac becomes eleventh Inca.*

1519   *Cortés conquers the Aztecs in Mexico.*

1521   *Portuguese adventurer Aleixo de Garcia the first European to set foot in Inca empire.*

1522   *Spanish exploration of the Peruvian coast begins.*

1525   *Tahuantinsuyo struck by unknown epidemic, killing Huayna Capac and many others; Huascar becomes twelfth Inca.*

1529   *Francisco Pizarro granted 'capitulación' to conquer Peru.*

Spanish Conquest

1532   *Atahualpa defeats Huascar to become the thirteenth Inca. May: Francisco Pizarro and conquistadors land at Tumbez. November: capture of Inca Atahualpa at Cajamarca.*

1533   *July: Incas pay Atahualpa's ransom of a room full of gold, Atahualpa executed. November: Pizarro enters Cusco. December: coronation of puppet Manco Inca.*

1534   *23 March: Pizarro founds the Spanish city of Cusco.*

1535   *6 January: Pizarro founds Lima as capital city.*

1536   *May: Cusco burned by native rebels in Manco Inca's Great Rebellion; Spanish recapture Sacsayhuaman.*

1537   *April: Diego de Almagro seizes Cusco and begins civil war. July: Paullu appointed Inca by Diego de Almagro; Manco Inca retreats to Cordillera Vilcabamba and founds independent state.*

1538   *April: Almagro defeated in battle of Las Salinas and executed.*

1539   *July: Great Rebellion finally suppressed with invasion of Vilcabamba. November: execution of native commanders at Yucay and capture of Manco Inca's wife Cura Ocllo, then murdered by Francisco Pizarro.*

1541   *Francisco Pizarro murdered in Lima by former supporters of Almagro.*

1542   *'New laws on the Indies' promulgated by Spanish crown, seeking to limit powers of conquistadors.*

1544   *June/July: Manco Inca murdered by Spanish fugitives. October: Gonzalo Pizarro rebels, takes Lima.*

1548   *April: Gonzalo Pizarro defeated and executed.*

1557   *October: Spanish tempt Inca Sayri Tupac out of Vilcabamba for Cusco; his brother Titu Cusi takes over.*

1569   *November: Viceroy de Toledo arrives in Lima.*

1571   *May: Death of Titu Cusi in Vilcabamba, accession of Tupac Amaru.*

1572   *June: Vilcabamba finally destroyed by army of Viceroy de Toledo. September: Tupac Amaru, last true Inca, executed in Cusco. Economic exploitation, epidemics of measles, smallpox, influenza, etc. have now reduced the native population to a fraction of its previous level.*

Colonial Era

1650   *Colonial buildings of Cusco destroyed by earthquake – Inca buildings survive unharmed; rebuilding starts.*

17thC   *Cusco school of art develops.*

1673   *November: Bishop Mollinedo arrives in Cusco; painting and decorative religious arts flourish under his patronage.*

Further Reading

18thC	Cusco becomes a major centre of painting and decorative religious arts.
1742, 1750	Native rebellions suppressed; brutal reprisals against rural population.
1780	Inca noble Tupac Amaru killed after unsuccessful native revolt. Further reprisals follow.
1814	Spanish settlers begin insurrection against rule of Spanish king.
	Independence
1821	Peruvian independence proclaimed by San Martín; Viceroy retreats to Cusco, which becomes, briefly, the capital.
1824	Battles of Junin and Ayacucho end colonial rule; little change for general population.
1824–90	Prolonged instability: Guano Boom lasts 40 years until Nitrate Boom triggers Pacific War with Chile, in which Peru loses territory to Chile. Peru bankrupt.
1890	'Peruvian Corporation' formed to rescue the economy; limited prosperity follows for the controlling elite.
1911	July: American archaeologist Hiram Bingham discovers the ruins of Machu Picchu. August: goes on to discover sites at Vitcos and Espíritu Pampa.
1919	Native rebellions and general strike reflect the poor conditions of the general population; repressive counter-measures prevent unrest spreading.
1924	APRA (American Popular Revolutionary Alliance) founded.
1932	APRA uprising put down; atrocities by military government follow.
1940/41	American expedition clears the 'Inca Trail', discovering sites of Huiñay Huayna and Intipata.
1950	Cusco hit by major earthquake; many colonial buildings lost.
1964/65	American archaeologist Gene Savoy excavates Espíritu Pampa and identifies the site as Vilcabamba, last stronghold of the Incas.
1968	Progressive military government of General Velasco seizes power and carries out land and other reforms but without lasting success.
1980	Sendero Luminoso (Shining Path) insurgents launch first military action, in department of Ayacucho.
1985	Alan García elected first APRA president, fails to carry out effective reform. Economic crisis and hyper-inflation rapidly erode living standards. Much of Peru, including Lima, disrupted by Sendero Luminoso and repressive military counter-measures; widespread atrocities on both sides.
1988	Major right-wing parties amalgamate; well-known author M. Vargas Llosa emerges as favourite for right-wing presidential nomination. Inflation at 2,000%.
1989	Civil war intensifies in many areas; Cusco region remains generally calm. Economic crisis deepens, Alan García universally unpopular.
1990	Presidential elections to be held.

History and Culture

The Ancient Civilizations of Peru, *J. Alden Mason, Pelican Books, London, 1968. Describes pre-Inca civilizations as well as Inca, emphasis on early history and culture.*

The Incas of Peru, *Sir Clements Markham, Librerias ABC, Lima, 1977 (first published 1910). A fascinating series of essays, mainly about the Incas (some pre-Inca), into the Conquest era.*

The Conquest of the Incas, *John Hemming, Penguin Books, London, 1987. The definitive modern account of the Conquest; enjoyable and vital background reading.*

History of the Conquest of Peru, *William Prescott, New York, 1847 (and subsequent editions). The original classic account of the Conquest.*

Lost City of the Incas, *Hiram Bingham, New York, 1948. The explorer's melodramatic account of the discovery of Machu Picchu, which he believed to be Vilcabamba.*

Royal Commentaries of the Incas, *Garcilaso de la Vega. Vol I, Lisbon, 1609; Vol II, Cordoba, 1617, trans Harold V. Livermore, London, 1966.*

Guide Books

Exploring Cusco, *Peter Frost, Bradt Enterprises (England); Lima 2000 (Peru), 1989. Probably the fullest guide to the Cusco region; good pocket format.*

Peru – A Travel Survival Kit, *Rob Rachowieki, Lonely Planet Publications, Australia & California, 1987.*

The Budget Traveller's Guide to Peru, *John Forrest (self published), 64 Belsize Park, London NW3. Useful booklet full of practical information, updated annually.*

Cusco – Guia Turistica, *Lima 2000, 1988. Pocket-sized booklet worth buying for its maps alone.*

F 7/25/95